toward the goal

Stories of Faith, God & Hockey

www.hockeyministries.org

Author, Cathy Ellis is a communications professional, writer, an avid hockey fan, and is honoured to have been invited by Hockey Ministries International to be a part of bringing this book to you. She currently works for Focus on the Family, a non-profit family help ministry – and she shares HMI's passion to encourage hockey players and their families with the message of hope found in Jesus Christ. Cathy lives in Parker, Colorado with her husband, Mathew. They have been married for 23 years, and have two wonderful daughters, Maddie and Carley.

Design Concept by b² Retail Solutions

Production by John LeBrun

NHL action photos by Getty Images

Youth and family photos provided by the featured players

Hockey Ministries International thanks the players featured in this book for their willingness to share their personal stories of faith in Jesus Christ.

Thanks as well to all who contributed to the development of this book in writing, editing, coordinating interviews, reviewing manuscripts, researching data, locating photos, developing design concepts and producing the final product.

contents

Introduction by

Mike Gartner

Here is a book packed with the inspiring life stories *of eight NHL hockey players. Some of these players share stories of victory in the face of adversity; others focus on struggle alone, where victory is much more elusive. But one theme runs throughout the book: these are men for whom competitive hockey, its victories and its defeats, has served to strengthen their faith in the journey with Jesus Christ – Christ who is there with us through every struggle, through every victory and through every defeat – belief in a God who loves us.*

As the athletes in this book – David Booth, B.J. Crombeen, Shane Doan, Mike Fisher, Dan Hamhuis, Mike Rupp, Michael Sauer, and Doug Jarvis – engage at the highest level in the speed and excitement of this hard-hitting game, they experience the same everyday highs and lows that we do. Cheers quickly turn to boos. Performance on and off the ice is scrutinized by a demanding public. Like all of us, they pass some tests and fail others. And like all of us, they have needs and seek answers to the important questions of life.

My hockey career was the stuff of every young man's dreams. I started skating when I was three and played on my first team at the age of five. My midget team won the Wrigley Midget Hockey Championship, and as a teenager, I represented Canada in a tournament in Russia. I was drafted in the first round by the Washington Capitals in 1979, and scored 36 goals in my rookie season. I scored 30 or more goals in 17 of the 19 years I played, finishing my career in 1998 with a total of 708 goals, just the fifth player ever to reach the 700 goal plateau. In 2001, I was inducted into the Hockey Hall of Fame. But all of the material benefits that accompany hockey fame and fortune left me without answers to life's important questions.

In 1980, I met Jean Pronovost when he joined the Washington Capitals. Jean had played 13 seasons in the NHL and was a 50-goal scorer. His strength of character distinguished him on and off the ice, and as a fellow-right winger, he was willing to share his experience with me. Our friendship developed, and he and his wife, Diane, invited me to attend Bible studies in their home. Although I had attended church in my youth, I never really understood how, in our faith and with the help of the Bible, we can find answers to the important questions of life. As we studied the Bible, I began to realize that there was no middle ground.

Then, on a flight between games, Jean asked me simply, "Mike, if this plane goes down, do you know where you will spend eternity?" He explained to me how I could know and be assured of spending eternity in heaven with Christ. This assurance comes by accepting God's forgiveness made possible by Jesus' death on the cross, and by inviting Jesus to be my Saviour. On that same road trip, in the quietness of my hotel room, I got on my knees and said, "Lord if you are real, come into my life now and change me." I found peace... a peace that profoundly impacted the rest of my life. I knew that God was in control of every situation. My faith helped me to handle the highs and the lows of the game – the injuries and trades, the scoring sprees and the slumps – and of life. I knew then that God had a plan for my life.

And, I was more motivated than ever. I played to glorify God, and I played my best. I felt responsible to God to use the talents and abilities He had given me. My new found faith not only made me a better athlete, it made me a better person.

As you read this book and learn about the underlying Christian faith of each of these players, my hope is that, as I did, you too will encounter Christ – and with Him, a new peace and a new, strong and positive perspective on the game of life.

David Booth

Dave hoists the Mason Cup,
as a member of MSU CCHA league champions 2006.

David, age 4

David with brothers Matt and Joe

David with Dad, Mike Booth

"Not now." "Wait." *Words none of us like to hear, especially when the pieces of life seem to be coming together and moving in the right direction. We've all experienced them – sometimes from parents, teachers, or employers. But for David Booth, they came in the form of a 5'11" 195-pound center iceman, right in the prime of his career, when he least expected it. This wasn't how the dream of playing in the NHL was supposed to turn out.*

Like many hockey players growing up in Detroit, Michigan, David dreamed of playing in the NHL, but never imagined that he would beat the astronomical odds of making it. He played in college at Michigan State and went through the typical soul-searching of a student trying to discover what he was meant to do. "I kept switching my major, four or five times, trying to figure out what I was going to do when I graduated. I thought about becoming a dentist, because that's what my dad was. I took one semester of classes, and realized that was not for me. I had so many doubts and I never thought I was good enough. I had a couple of years in college where I didn't play well at all, so I just kept switching my major to try to find a career that I liked."

Little did David know that, in spite of his searching, a plan had already been laid out for him. He signed a minor league contract and was happy with a place on the 4th line. With great teammates, he was thankful to be playing and doing what he loved.

The first time he was called up to the NHL, he was in Rochester in the minors. "I never expected the call. Playing on the 4th line, I never thought I'd have a chance. When I got that call in November, I couldn't believe it. After playing three games, I thought, 'This is so cool – this is what you dream of!'" David went back down to the minors for a few more games before being called back up, where he stayed from January, 2006 all the way through the rest of the year. He was only playing 5 – 10 minutes per game, but he was in the NHL – just trying to make it. The following season, he played the whole year – recording 22 goals and 18 assists – before he realized that just maybe he could make it in the NHL.

And make it he did. Since 2006, as a left wing for the Florida Panthers and then the Vancouver Canucks, David has tallied 89 goals and 86 assists, for 174 points – not bad for a guy who thought he should be a dentist. But, while making it in the NHL comes with all of the fame and fortune and glory you'd expect, it doesn't come without its own set of challenges and trials...which brings us back to that 5'11" 195-pound center iceman.

Training for Life with David Booth: A favorite verse

David is particularly drawn to the Psalms and encouraged by scripture about the young shepherd, David, who eventually became King of Israel. Here are a few that have been most meaningful to him:

Psalm 84:10: *"Better is one day in your courts than a thousand elsewhere..."* That's one of my favorites. I've been to so many places in this world – I get to travel and do a lot of things, whether that's hunting, golfing, traveling, visiting friends in different places. But nothing I'm doing on this earth is going to compare with time I spend alone with Christ and walking with Him. That speaks to me a lot, and shows how awesome it is to be a Christian, and know the love He has for you. I think so many people try to get their satisfaction from so many different things, and they don't realize how great it is to just spend some alone time with God – I think that's very key.

On October 24, 2009, David took a hit from Philadelphia Flyers' Mike Richards that left him unconscious and required him to be taken off the ice on a stretcher. The hit was so big, it even caught the attention of NHL general managers, who, as a result, unanimously recommended a rule change to ban hits to the head. But for David, it marked a very big "wait – not now" in his run toward his goals. "That's one of the hardest things I've gone through, because it affected my life, my career – everything. I was fired up about the Olympics. Making the Olympic team was a huge goal of mine. I wanted to have a good year and make the playoffs, but that was all taken away from me." David had gone up against a tough opponent, and the opponent stopped him dead in his tracks – or his skates, as the case may be.

Some people might be tempted to fall back on their anger, and blame and rail against the person who stopped them from achieving their dreams, or become obsessed with reliving the scene to see how it could have been avoided. Some people might, but David fell back on something else – the strength of his faith, which had been planted when he was just a kid and had been growing, tested and challenged, throughout his career. As it turned out, the Richards hit presented one of the biggest challenges David had ever faced, and caused him to look at the whole of his life, and make some key decisions based on where he had come from, and where he was going – particularly where his faith was concerned. What did he believe? Was it for real? And how could it help him now?

Like many kids who grow up in a Christian home, going to church and Sunday school, David learned all of the stories and appreciated the strong foundational values his parents had instilled in him. It wasn't until college, though, that everything changed for him. The whole freshman hockey team lived in a dorm together, and one night the second week of school, two guys invited David to attend an Athletes in Action Bible study with them. He thought, "these guys are my teammates, and I could use some prayer right now, so, yeah, I'll go." From then on, he began meeting one-on-one with the Athletes in Action director, Phil Gillespie. After Phil had mentored David for some time, he asked him a simple but profound question, "Are you going to Heaven when you die?" David knew the answer was "Yes" because he believed in God, had faith in Him, and he believed that Christ died on the cross for his sins. But he also knew in his heart that the way he was living did not reflect his beliefs, and things had to change.

Training for Life with David Booth: A favorite verse

Romans 1:16: *"I am not ashamed of the Gospel..."* That is another one that has stuck with me, and I wish I could live this out more. I think we sometimes get a little timid around certain people or act a certain way, but we have to be bold in those situations, and that's a good reminder that there's no reason to be ashamed. This one is pretty big for me – not having fear, because it can be a hard thing to do. I think people are drawn to people with passion. If you have a sense of conviction and people can see it in you, people will be drawn to that. That's how Paul lived, and that's how we ought to live – not ashamed of the Gospel, but letting your faith show through.

David experienced the turnaround he needed at a camp in Colorado. "After my freshman year of college, it really made sense to me. Now I knew I needed to become a Christian and live what I believed. For the longest time, I believed in God, but there was no fruit of that. I wasn't anything, just an average person, going to school, working on hockey. That's what defined my life. But that changed when I went to that Athletes in Action Ultimate Camp in Colorado. I realized that walking through life as a phony or pretending to be what you're not is a sad place to live. I think a lot of people do it. It kind of made sense to me at that camp. I understood the real love of Christ, that he really did die for me and everything I've done, and he wants to be my friend. That's what made the change in me so quick. Once you feel that, it will change your life. It's not just a set of rules you have to live by – it's understanding how much He loved me, and that was really cool. I had to follow His lead after that."

As he began a new life that could require him to go against the flow of popular culture, David didn't go it alone. He credits a number of key influencers who came alongside him, providing encouragement and inspiration. Obviously, Phil Gillespie with Athletes in Action played a tremendous role, as did his parents for the foundation they laid. "I met John Vanbiesbrouck in college. Growing up, watching him play, I thought he was awesome. That's who I looked up to, and when I found out he was a Christian, it was an inspiration for me. Now that I've moved on from college and have been active in professional hockey for a few years, I continue to grow and get stronger. I would not be where I am today if it weren't for the people who continue to pile into my life. I've had so many good talks with good athletes. My best teammate who really encouraged me was Noah Welch. He really got me fired up again too. He was my roommate on the road, and the Bible studies we did on the road were an encouragement." David also draws strength from his pastor, Bob Coy, Hockey Ministries International chaplain, Jerry Sander, and special friends, like HMI NHL Chapel Coordinator, Tim Burke and his wife, Christine. He can't emphasize enough the importance of surrounding himself with people who share his faith and hold him accountable for "bearing the fruit" of that faith. It not only helps him to grow, it also energizes him. "We had five or six guys (on the Panthers) who would come out to check out what chapel's all about. It's fun to be a part of that, when you've got other athletes who show an interest in growing spiritually and helping each other out."

True help, like these true teammates, mentors, and friends, are especially important in any walk of life, not only in times of adversity like the one David would eventually face, but also in helping him handle some of the pressures and temptations he faces as an NHL star. Receiving sudden fame and fortune, while sounding like a great problem to have, can take its toll on young players. How many stories have we seen in tabloids and magazines about athletes and other stars who received too much too fast and weren't prepared to handle the demands of being an instant celebrity? Many end up throwing their lives away on drugs, gambling, and every sort of out of control behavior, all of which David has seen. "Struggles?" he says, "There are tons! There are always opportunities to go out. The temptations are very real, and dealing with them can be tough." Not to say that David hasn't made mistakes or taken a few missteps. After all, he is an easy-going guy who tries to look for the best in everyone, and, he admits, this may have gotten him in some trouble where ulterior motives have been involved. But he's learning to draw a line between isolating himself from certain situations where he'd rather not be, and meeting people where they are and trying to show them the love of Christ. "I mess up every day with the sins I struggle with, so I'm not one to judge. That's where prayer comes in. That's really the only way through it, along with having a good support system. The people who have been a big part of my life are the people who have kept me grounded and accountable for staying on the right path."

Being aware of temptation and keeping the right perspective also helps, especially in a setting that's almost entirely dedicated to seeing a team of players' dreams come true. As David acknowledges, "Just staying humble is a big challenge. Everything we do is geared toward us. Everyone's job is to serve

How Does He Do That? David's Special Training Tips

What do you think is the best way to train?

David: Everyone's training more – it's becoming more a part of the game, so now you have to work out off-ice to complement your on-ice skills and make them better. A lot of people think, "I'm going to go to the weight room to get bigger and stronger" – even kids who are 14, 15, even 12 or 13-year-olds are going to the weight room thinking they're going to get better. I'd strongly disagree with that, because I think when you're that age, you just need to let your body grow, and not worry about that. As you get to be 16, 17, your body starts adapting – as you become a young man, your body will change, and you'll start to grow and get stronger naturally. But if you're a kid growing up, I'd strongly recommend going through plyometrics, or going to a track at your school, and working on quick speed, because the game is becoming so quick. Some of the best players in the NHL right now are small – they're not necessarily the guys who are big, but those who can skate and use their agility to get away from the big guys. So, I'd stick to the track and working on quick feet, trying to get explosive power from doing a lot of jumping, versus just sitting in the weight room and doing arm curls, which really have no place in today's hockey.

Also, in the off-season, I'm not a big fan of scrimmaging. I'd rather work on a few skills than just get out there and skate around. Once you get into the season, you're always in practice and games, so I like to work on more specific skills in the summer.

us. While we're playing hockey, we have trainers who look out for us, equipment guys who take care of us, weight trainers who focus only on us. When we travel, we have people who serve us on airplanes and hotels. Everyone's always serving us, and it's hard to receive that and not take it for granted. It's even harder to reverse that and ***be*** a servant. That's a struggle of mine for sure – just trying to be more of a servant. I mean, it's nice when people serve you, but we're called to be servants. Jesus washed the feet of his disciples, and I think that's something I need to do more – to take time and be that example of Christ, and be a servant."

Training for Life with David Booth: A favorite verse

Psalm 34:18: *"The Lord is close to the brokenhearted and saves those who are crushed in spirit."* This was a big one when I was going through my injury. Everyone goes through those times when they become brokenhearted, when they feel crushed and down and they're at rock bottom. But that's also when the Lord is closest to you, and when you're going to learn the most about Him and about yourself too.

This perspective isn't just talk for David Booth. He also sees his success and high profile as a way to give back to others and put into practice what he has learned along his journey. "Maybe that's why I'm in the NHL – to keep sharing my faith with people who are drawn to me because I'm a pro. I think my job is to be a light to my teammates and share what Jesus has done in my life. I've done a lot of the summer hockey camps with Hockey Ministries International, and even though it's somewhat of a sacrifice to take time out of my training schedule to go, I'm sure God's hand is leading me to do this. I went overseas to a camp, and seeing these kids in foreign countries and the passion they have – when I left there knowing I had an impact on these kids and seeing kids come to Christ – that's as good as it gets!"

Training for Life with David Booth:
A favorite verse

1 Samuel 16:7: *"...The Lord does not look at the things man looks at. Man looks at the outward appearance, but the Lord looks at the heart."* I personally love that because, especially in today's culture, everything is so superficial. Let's talk about how God looks at the heart – you know your heart, and there's no faking it with God. That's really cool.

As for the game of hockey, as good as it gets for David is giving it all he has and playing with all the speed and scoring ability for which he's known. Hard work, discipline and determination have been his constant companions throughout his career, as have exceptional teammates and maybe even a little help from above. "Goal scoring comes with playing with really good players. I'm playing with the best players in the NHL, and I'm able to do what I do because our skills complement each other. But once I had half a season that went really well. Honestly, I'm not lying when I say this, but it was all God – because I couldn't believe some of the goals I scored were going in! I asked, 'What's going on here?' I think it was just Him saying, 'Hey, this is where you need to be. This is my plan for you.' That's the way I look at it because I know I'm not skilled enough on my own to be here. Like when David went up against Goliath, no one expected him to win at all, and yet he had God on his side. I don't come with the best skill set, just like David didn't come with the biggest sword or the strongest shield.

He just went with the word of God, and in a sense, I think that's how I play the game today – God, let your will be done out there."

The obvious question is, how can God's will be done in such a physically aggressive game? Does He really intend for players to hit each other, fight, and sometimes even get hurt? As one who's been on the receiving end of pain, David has some clear thoughts about this as well. "If you look in the Old Testament, you see so many battle stories, and so many warriors. And when people think of a "Christian," they might think of a wimp, or someone who's timid and can't be physical or push the limits, up to the line. But when you look at the Christian hockey players, you see some of the hardest working, most feared guys, and even some of the best fighters in the NHL. That's part of the sport, and there's a place for it. I think you can see the passion some of these Christians have in the way they play the game. I don't think they're beating someone up because they absolutely hate the guy. It's more for the love of the game and commitment to their teammates. That's what makes them play the best they can. That's where you see the enthusiasm and passion coming out – playing the game physical because that's the way it's supposed to be played. You have to be strong. We work hard and train our bodies for the physical nature of the game, and it's just a way to give glory back to God. The guys I look up to, like Mike Fisher, you see his faith, and he's one of the hardest players to play against. He finishes every check, he fights, and that's something any little kid growing up watching the game can say, 'I want to be like that guy,' because of the way he plays, with Christ in his life. I played with another Christian this year, Darcy Hordichuk. He's a tough competitor, and a fighter. He would go to church with me, and chapels, and give encouragement to me. That was so great to see, that there are Christians out there who have passion and use the game of hockey to glorify God."

Passion is great, but David also knows what it's like to get caught up in a game and let emotions run wild. Some players just write off these times, saying "it's just a part of the game," but David uses these times as learning opportunities. "Everyone has those times when actions are based on emotion. But as you start to recognize it and situations where you shouldn't have acted a certain way, the next time it happens, you can usually tell yourself to calm down and let it work itself out. A lot of times, when you react on emotion, it's usually the wrong way. But when you have a clear head, and you can think about it and prepare for it, you continue to learn."

How Does He Do That?
David's Special Training Tips

What routines do you have?

David: I always do at least 45 minutes of a warm-up. I think a warm-up is really key, so you don't get injuries by jumping into a workout right away. That includes stretching, doing some short sprints, doing some shuffles – just so your body is moving. After about 45 minutes of warming up, then I do a pretty standard 45 minute work-out. I think an hour and a half is plenty of time to get everything in. The one thing I do that might be a little different is a lot of one-leg training, like skating on one leg. That's very hard to do, but I think that's the game – you're always on one foot or the other. I think that's really big.

Preparation is the key – knowing these times will come and intentionally preparing for them. David doesn't hesitate in crediting prayer for his ability to gain self-control. He prays before every game, and even between his 50 or 55 second shifts on the bench. "You've got to keep thinking about what you're doing, and you have to be prepared to battle and give 100 percent. But there are things that come up – maybe, you have a bad shift – you might get down on yourself and feel you let your teammates down, and lose your temper because you want to do better. That's when you have to be able to say to yourself, 'calm down, everyone makes mistakes. Just relax. Keep your head where it needs to be, and keep that focal point.'"

How Does He Do That? David's Special Training Tips

What do you work on to help you become a better goal-scorer?

David: I work with a couple of specific coaches – a skating coach, to help my speed, and a stick-handling coach. Speed is important because I think most of my goals come from beating someone to the net. I don't think my puck skills are necessarily the best out there, but I work really hard on being good enough. I don't think they're ever going to be as good as a Pavel Datsyuk out there – that guy can really move the puck around! He's just so good, to have defense all around and keep the puck on his stick. That's a rare talent. I also work on shooting a lot of pucks so I can continue to develop that skill.

Cameras only add to the pressure – with every mistake, every tantrum, every emotion captured for all time, and broadcast for all the world to see, sometimes replayed over and over. Like, for example, big hits on star players.

Do an internet search on "David Booth, NHL," and immediately after the obvious NHL sites and stats, are entry after entry on David's injuries and the danger of head shots in the NHL.

The infamous hit on David is well documented, as is his recovery – followed some two months later with another hit that knocked him unconscious and caused him to sit out the remainder of the 2009/2010 season. David was able to return for the entire 2010/2011 season, though he finished with an impressive 23 goals and 17 assists, for 40 points.

Training for Life with David Booth: A favorite verse

Luke 12:48: *"...From everyone who has been given much, much will be required..."* Everyone wants it all, but it's not that easy – there's a lot of responsibility that comes with the talents God grants us. All of our talents may not be the same, but what He's given us, we have to use and not let those talents go to waste. That's always been one of my favorites – to realize the responsibility to use the talents He's given me – and sometimes it's hard work! I think some people might give up on their talents too easily, and say, "that's just not for me because it's too hard, and I don't like it." But if you have a gift, God wants you to use it – so don't give up on it just because it's hard.

Even with a bright future stretched out before him, David still thinks about the Richards hit and hopes he will never forget what he learned during his recovery. "When you go through tough times, that's when you think about your life more, and you kind of wonder what it's all about. If everything's good, you sometimes don't think you have a need for God, and that's a very bad spot to be in. You just go through life living your emotions, but when you have something taken away from you, you start to question a lot of things. Even with the injuries and losing what I loved, I know I don't go through some of the struggles a lot of people go through – fighting in a war for your country or losing a loved one. But everyone has struggles in their lives, and this was mine. It was very personal."

Training for Life with David Booth: A favorite verse

Psalm 51:10: *"Create in me a pure heart, O God, and renew a steadfast spirit within me."* I have to say that one every day – *every day* – "create in me a pure heart." It's a great verse for a fresh start. I think we go through times when we might have slipped a little bit, or fallen, or drifted away from God for a little bit. I think everyone does. But what a verse! To say, "create in me a pure heart." God gives us a second chance and a third chance. He's always there, and this verse is the way he says it…every morning.

David recalls that fateful night, lying in a hospital bed, wondering if he would ever play hockey again. He remembers he did not wallow in self-pity or despair, but found comfort in the promises of God and in the struggles of another David, who lived and wrote some 3000 years ago – the same words that continue to strengthen him today. "You know, just looking at David when he wrote some of the Psalms, he was a wild man! He was a guy who was living in the desert, he didn't have food or much of anything, but he was very relational with God, like he was questioning Him. At the end of almost every Psalm, though, he would praise God, and say His ways are holy. It just put my little problems into perspective to know that God has all the power and that He can do everything was very soothing to my soul, a comfort. Sometimes you don't see His picture in the moment, but it's more than you could ever imagine. That's why, when I went through what I went through, I had to start writing down what I was reading, because I never want to forget what I was going through and what brought me through that tough time. It was a big time for me, to continue to develop in my faith.

"Don't get me wrong, I was angry too, but the Bible says, 'in your anger, do not sin;' it doesn't say, 'do not get angry.' Everyone gets angry. I think that's a natural emotion that we have. David wrote about his enemies and asked God why He didn't just smite them. I used to think that was crazy! But he just shared what his feelings were, and talked to God like a normal friend, which is a way to get closer to God. That's why, whenever I need a good read, or am going through a struggle, or even a praise, I think the Psalms cover it all."

So what appeared to David as his greatest challenge at the time actually led to one of the most significant growing times of his life. It certainly changed his perspective on what it means to "have it all." He might say that having dreams and goals and passion is important to pursue the desires that are in our hearts, whether that's going to the Olympics or becoming a dentist. He would most certainly say that the journey toward our goal is equally, if not more, important as the goal itself, especially if we're living lives of eternal consequence, with the courage it takes to follow Christ. "I'd say we're not on this earth to have comfort. I think a lot of people are always searching for the best, most comfortable, easiest, get-rich-quick life, but that's not what this life is about. It's about sacrifice. You see the ultimate sacrifice in Christ, and we need to take after His example. As you start to understand the love that Christ has for us, that's what changes your life. If you want to be successful, this is the way to be successful. I remember someone telling me that everyone dies, and their whole life is summed up in the little dash between the year they were born and the year they died. It's never going to say how many goals I scored, or how many games I won, how many friends I had or how much money I had. But when you're living a life for Christ, and you're going to get to go to Heaven, that means something for the whole time you're on earth. When people can look back and say, 'man, that guy changed some lives, that guy was a God-fearing man,' that's what I want to be remembered for. That's why we're on earth – to prepare for eternity."

"Restore to me the joy of your salvation and grant me a willing spirit, to sustain me." Psalm 51:12

David Booth

Based on David's story and favorite scriptures, spend some time reflecting on your own story and asking these questions:

1. What's your dream? Which people have helped you to see and pursue your dream? How has David's story inspired you to keep going on the journey toward your goal?
2. What are your specific talents? How has David's story helped you view your talents and encouraged you to use them?
3. Have you ever experienced unexpected adversity? How did you handle it? What struck you most about David's experience with adversity?
4. What kinds of struggles are you currently going through? How might David's story or perspectives help you deal with these struggles?
5. What encouraged you most about David's story? What could you relate to the most, and how might some of David's experiences and perspectives apply to your situation?
6. Is Christ a part of your life? What would you say if David's mentor asked you the same question he asked David, "Are you going to Heaven when you die?" What would your answer be?

David, 10 yrs old getting his 1st bow for his birthday

2010 with Red Stag from New Zealand

Home after the Panther Season ended

David on a mountain climbing trip

David skiing with brothers Matt and Joel in Aspen

David with brother Joel on a Hockey Ministry trip

Family vacation in Rome

B.J. Crombeen
EASTON

Brandon James, 6 months

Brandon James, 4 yrs

Brandon's first time on skates, 2 yrs – Dec. 1987 (Denver, Colorado)

Brandon James, 5 yrs

Following in your father's footsteps *can be a real honor for many young men – a rewarding badge of accomplishment, as one generation passes the baton to the next. But how many young men can say the baton handed to them was a career in the National Hockey League, playing for the same team, and even wearing the same number as their dad? B.J. Crombeen can.*

Though he retired from hockey the year B.J. was born, Mike Crombeen obviously passed the love of the game on to his sons, both of whom played hockey from a young age. As B.J. reminisces, "I have an older brother who's five years older than I am, and a sister who's three years older, so I was the youngest growing up. We moved to Sarnia, Ontario when I was three-years-old, and I spent most of my childhood there. Obviously, having an older brother playing hockey, I was always chasing him around, trying to keep up with him. And with my dad having played, hockey was a big thing in my family, and playing hockey in Canada was a big thing – everyone kind of did that."

B.J. also followed in his father's footsteps of faith – along a journey that would take him from a comfortable home and family through the hills and valleys of becoming a professional hockey player, all the while coming to realize that he wasn't walking alone. "My dad was involved with Hockey Ministries International, and I grew up in a Christian family who went to church and had a strong faith. When I was thirteen or fourteen, we moved to Newmarket, and I played hockey there for a few years. Then I was drafted by the Barrie Colts in the Ontario Hockey League, and I moved off to Barrie when I was sixteen. This was the first time I lived by myself, and I definitely had some years where I wandered away from my faith. I still had the faith background, but I wasn't living the active faithful life. When I came to the Colts, I was just a young kid trying to fit in and not step on anyone's toes. When you're still living at home, you're not faced with as many challenges – but when you move away as a sixteen year old and you're going to a different school, meeting new people, and playing at a totally different level of hockey, you obviously go through a lot of ups and downs. This is when I started to drift away.

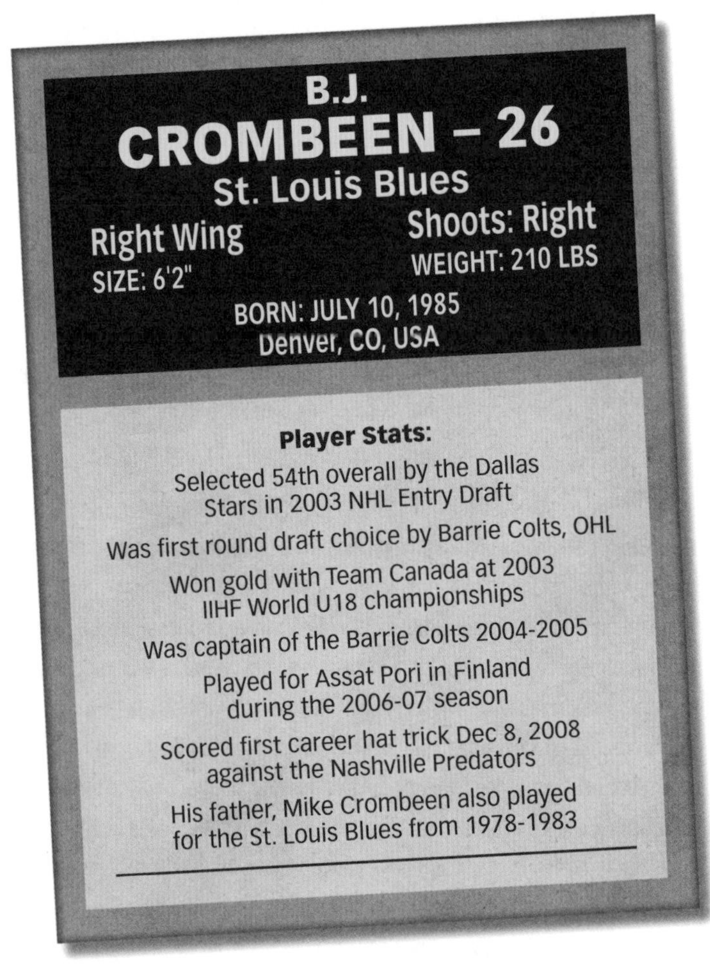

"The biggest challenge for me was that I've always been a person who likes to be in control, whether it's in hockey or in life. Many situations were very trying and frustrating for me to go through – everything from how much ice time I was getting, to who I was playing with, to living away from home and trying to deal with all of the different challenges of being on my own at such a young age. I think it was in my second year in Barrie when I was going through those 'downs' that I started to see how little control I had of things. I started to realize that something was missing, and I needed faith in my life. It was through the Hockey Ministries International chapel program that I got reacquainted with my faith. The biggest realization for me was that I could either beat myself up over every little thing, or I could trust in the Lord and know He has everything in control, and that I could live and work for Him instead of trying to control everything myself. Through the chapel program, I had people to talk to about what I was experiencing, and I also met my girlfriend, now wife Janet, during this time. The chaplain was the pastor of a local church in Barrie, so we started going there. As I was hearing different things and seeing different things about trusting in Jesus Christ, I started to think more about what all of that meant. Even then, though, I wasn't a hundred percent committed. It was more of a growth thing and it took me a while to come to the realization that I couldn't do everything myself and I couldn't control everything and write my own path. I had to trust in God, work my hardest, and try to do what I could, but just put it in God's hands. So, once I realized that with a relationship with Jesus, you can trust that He has everything under control, and all you have to do is go out and put your best foot forward whether it's your plan or not, Janet and I both recommitted our lives to the Lord, and we spent my last two years in junior trusting in Him. It's a daily thing I have to remind myself of, even now. But going through challenges by yourself is a lot more difficult than going through them with the Lord and having faith that He has all of those things under control."

How Does He Do That?
B.J.'s Special Training Tips

What special things do you do that make you the player you are?

B.J.: Once you work your way up the ladder in any pro sport, there's obviously talent and guys who work very hard to get where they are. But I also try to keep the mindset that my dad instilled in me fairly early that you have to be ready, willing, and able to outwork the guy you're competing against. Whether you've been in the NHL for a long time or you're just breaking in, there's always someone who wants to take your job and bump you out of your spot. So in both on and off the ice training, you have to be committed and willing to work that much harder than everyone else.

B.J. would find himself relying on the strength of his faith more and more as he approached his dream of playing in the NHL. "From Barrie, I was drafted by the Dallas Stars in 2003, and came up through their system. My first few years as a pro were fairly difficult years. I came in, and I played mostly in the American League, and a little bit in the East Coast League, but I didn't play a ton in my first year. It was a typically challenging first year as a pro, where things didn't really go as planned. And it was a huge adjustment period, moving on to play with men instead of teenagers."

During this time, B.J. learned the value of having a support system and being surrounded by those who could provide encouragement early in a career – especially for a young Christian facing the unpredictability of pro hockey. He built a solid foundation of support in the AHL, when he played for the Iowa Stars in the 2005-2006 season, and came under the wing of teammates Mike Smith and Dan Ellis. "You go through lots of highs and lows every season, and there are points where you begin to doubt yourself – whether you're going to be here, how long you're going to be here, where you're going with it. That's definitely where my faith has come in and really carried me through those times. It was a big thing for me, being a younger guy just coming into the league. I was twenty one when I went to Iowa, and just having guys there like Mike and Dan who could help us find a church and get involved in different things was so encouraging. They had both played pro for four or five years, so they had been through the different experiences of a pro hockey player's season. It was encouraging for me to have guys like that who were able to show me the ropes at a different level. We also had a chapel group there in Iowa, and when you have some of the older guys behind something like that, it makes it a lot easier for the younger guys to get involved without being intimidated.

"In the 2006-2007 season, I went over to Finland and played for a while over there, which was an interesting experience. Looking back, I think it was great from a hockey standpoint to live in a different culture. And then, I came back and actually finished up the season in the East Coast Hockey League. We ended up winning the championship, so it was a pretty neat experience to be able to do that.

"Then, in my third year pro, I went back to the American League, and started off similarly to my first year. I wasn't really playing much, and things weren't really going as planned, so it was a tough year. I was kind of struggling, and this was a time when my faith really helped me. I just said to myself, 'I'm still going to continue to work hard and I'm still going to push myself.' I still really had to learn how to trust in God at a time like that, when I didn't know what was happening or where it might go. I started looking at other options and different things I might do if hockey wasn't going to work out. At the same time, I was still working hard, and I was still fully committed to playing hockey. It was always something I believed I could do, and I don't think you can ever really count yourself out if you're working hard. At the same time, I was trusting in God and just letting Him lead me on the path of where I was going to go. That was also the year I got engaged to Janet, at Christmas time.

Training for Life with B.J. Crombeen: A favorite verse

Philippians 4:13: *"I can do everything through him who gives me strength."* I think every person, no matter what they're doing, comes to times when they doubt themselves or they doubt whether they can do something, and this is one verse I constantly go back to. It gives me confidence that if the Lord has put me in a situation, I can do it and I can succeed at it – I'm going to have to work hard, but this is something I can lean on.

"Later that year, in January or February of 2008, I actually got called up to the NHL for my first game with Dallas. My mom, dad, fiancé, and brother were all able to make it to my first game, which was a pretty exciting experience. I finished the year going up and down, and the following year I started out in Dallas, played fifteen games, then was put on waivers. On November 18, 2008, I made the move to St. Louis to play for the Blues, and I've been there ever since. When I found out I was going to St. Louis, it was really exciting for me. Not only was I able to follow in my dad's footsteps and play hockey professionally, I was actually able to play for the same team, and even wear the same number. That's pretty special."

B.J. has had other special moments in his career with St. Louis, as he's carved out a role for himself as a physical player who stands up for his teammates. "I try to take pride in being a strong defensive player who plays a physical game, contributes on the penalty kill and in the last minutes of games, and I've been able to establish that I can be a reliable, defensive forward who can bring a physical element to the game.

"One of the best experiences was being able to make the playoffs in my first year with St. Louis. We had actually been in last place in the conference in February, and we were able to climb up and finish in sixth place. It was a short-lived playoff, and we got swept by Vancouver. Still, it was a pretty neat atmosphere going from being a team in the bottom of the standings, to clawing our way up together, working together and fighting to make it to the playoffs. That was a great experience, and something everyone who was a part of it really enjoyed. When I'm finished playing hockey and I look back on my career, that experience, as well as my first game and my first goal, will be something I'll cherish. I've also been privileged to have a real good group of teammates over the last few years, and the most rewarding part of my career has been the camaraderie and being able to be close with my teammates. A dream of mine was obviously to grow up and be able to play hockey for a living. I'm reminded every day, through the good times and the bad, that I'm pretty blessed to be able to do this. So I just try to enjoy every moment."

Riding through the good times and the bad times seems to be something B.J. Crombeen takes in stride in all areas of his life. Not only has he ridden the rollercoaster of uncertainty on the journey toward his goal, he has done so seamlessly managing a disease that might have put the brakes on a hockey career before it ever got started. When he was nine-years-old, B.J. was diagnosed with diabetes. Some kids, and their families, might be tempted to think that with the demands of controlling diabetes, sports would be difficult, if not impossible. B.J. takes another view. "When I first got diagnosed with diabetes, I didn't fully understand what it was or what was happening, but I had a lot of support from my friends and family. I remember when I was in the hospital and my brother and sister came in. One of the first things they brought me was an article about Bobby Clarke and how he had diabetes and played in the NHL. My philosophy was that diabetes is a pretty manageable disease, as long as you're willing to put in the time and effort. I think it's like anything else in life. You can choose to let it hold you back, or you can just deal with it and go on living your life. That has a lot to do with my parents, my family, and my friends who encouraged me and didn't let me give up. When I was in the early stages, I really had to decide whether I was going to let it hold me back or not, and they told me it's something I'm always going to have to deal with, and I'm going to have to just make the most of it and pay attention to it. People with this disease might have to do some things differently; they might have bad days with it, but it is what it is, and you just have to make the most of it. When I talk to diabetic kids, that's really the mindset I have. I try to tell them that it's something that does take time. It's not something everyone has to deal with, but it's pretty manageable if you do everything you have to do. I test my blood a lot, and I watch it pretty carefully. By doing that, it really doesn't affect me too much.

"It's actually opened up a lot of opportunities in the last few years for being able to talk about it and work with some charities. I hadn't really thought about it before, but now that I'm playing in the NHL, I can be a role model for younger kids. I've been able to meet people, either through the Juvenile Diabetes Foundation or other contacts here in St. Louis. People will come up to me and say, 'My son, or my nephew, is a diabetic, and he really looks up to you, that you can play at this level.' It's opened up a lot of doors to talk with people and encourage them that this isn't something that has to hold you back. You can make a choice to do anything you want with it."

How Does He Do That?
B.J.'s Special Training Tips

How do you approach your workouts?

B.J.: If I could give one bit of advice to anyone, I'd say you could do the exact same workout, and you could get a lot out of it, or a little out of it – just depending on how you approach it. My approach has always been to put everything I have into everything I do, and not ever step off the gas, or say, "I'm just going to take this one easy." Instead, I've always tried to say, "I'm going to put everything I have into this like it's my last workout," and I think that's really helped me to get a lot out of the training I do and helped me to be the best hockey player I can be.

Being a role model for kids with diabetes isn't just something B.J. talks about or hopes for from afar. He has also taken an active role in helping families understand the realities of the disease. "In the last few years, there have been several times when someone from our team or someone they know will invite a diabetic kid to come down to the locker room after a game, and I'll show them around the room and talk with them. Last year, we also started a charity called Crombeen for a Cure, to raise money for the St. Louis Juvenile Diabetes Research Foundation, and I've been meeting with other people who can help start a charity run here in St. Louis. There's been a lot of support, and it's been a lot of fun, being able to get involved in these events. A couple of years ago, I went to an event with several parents and young kids who were recently diagnosed, and just being able to talk with them was very rewarding. I got to share with them how I felt when I was first diagnosed with diabetes. I was pretty scared, and I wasn't sure about using needles and all of the other things that go along with it. At a younger age, kids can be embarrassed or nervous to tell others about their diabetes, and because of that, they often won't keep on top of it. So it's great when I can talk to them and say, 'It's nothing to be embarrassed about, and it's nothing to be shy about. It just is what it is, and you can really do anything you want with it."

B.J. also takes this same practical approach to living out his Christian faith, especially among teammates, and in an environment where hard-hitting, physical play and exemplifying Christ-like character may seem, on the surface, to be at odds with one another. But B.J. has no trouble reconciling his identity as a physical player and a Christian. "There have been a lot of physical and tough Christian hockey players who have come through the NHL, and in talking with them and listening to what they say, that's a role they take pride in – representing Christ by sticking up for their teammates and playing as hard as they can. If you've played the game, you understand there's a place for physical play or fighting, and that's what you're expected to do if you're put into that role. It's nothing personal; it's just part of the game. You don't necessarily have a grudge against someone or want to go after someone just to get them. It has more to do with the integrity of the game. Most of the players in the League have great respect for one another. You understand there are guys who are being asked to be those physical, aggressive players, and they're not going out trying to hurt anyone; it's just their role, and there's a common respect for that. There are times when a guy has someone in a situation where he could easily get him when he's down and out – but a large majority of the players do show respect for one another, because they know the tables could turn, and they could be in that same spot the next time. So showing respect for other players is really important.

Training for Life with B.J. Crombeen: A favorite verse

Proverbs 3:5-6: *"Trust in the Lord with all your heart and lean not on your own understanding; in all your ways acknowledge him, and he will make your paths straight."* I just keep coming back to realizing I don't have any control, and I need to trust in the Lord and trust in the plan He has for me. I can be sort of a stubborn person, and it took a lot of pounding until a lot of lessons in life really sunk in and I grasped that this is how I was going to live my life. Having that trust that He has a plan for me has helped me to stay a lot more even-keeled through the ups and downs, and even in my level of enjoyment. I just have to live it out and work my hardest at what I'm doing, and trust Him with the rest.

"**I think that just living a godly life every day**, being an honest person, putting others before yourself and making decisions based on your faith on a day to day basis, is the best way to demonstrate your faith to those around you. I'm not an overly vocal person, but I try to live out my faith by how I act and what I do daily. Whether you're a hockey player or working in an office, you're going to face different challenges. We all have to make decisions about how we're going to live our lives, and I just try to base my decisions on my faith. People may look at you a little differently, or they may try to get you to do things you don't believe in and you don't want to do, and you have to make that decision about whether you're going to do it or not. I don't think hockey is any different than any other area – you just have to make your decision and stand by it."

B.J. also knows he can't go it alone, and he continues to maintain relationships that help him keep his faith strong. "Obviously, having a strong faith at home, with my family and my wife, provides strong encouragement. My parents and brother and sister were a huge part of establishing my faith, right from the start, and they've also been behind me the whole way. Since starting my own family, with my wife and now having a little boy, the journey is a lot more enjoyable, and my faith means even more to me in everything I do. I've found that the love I have for my child, and realizing how much every little thing he does means to me, really puts the Lord's love for us into context. It's pretty amazing to think of how much the Lord loves us. I don't think we can ever really get a full grasp on it. Having a child definitely made me think a lot more about making sure I'm doing all I can to live the right life, to be an example, and to show him how to trust in the Lord. That's really inspired me. Hockey Ministries International has also done a lot of great things to encourage me – from the chapel programs to people I'm able to meet with when we go on the road, or when they come here to St. Louis, or talking on the phone and catching up through e-mail. Those things are always a source of reassurance."

Life, like hockey, may have its ups and downs, but through his experience, B.J. Crombeen has made a discovery that can carry him through all of the peaks and valleys. He believes it can help other young people as they ask the big questions, like *Do I have what it takes? What should I do with my life?* "The biggest thing that I've learned through the years is to really just put my trust and my life in the Lord's hands, and work hard at whatever I'm doing. I'm very blessed to be a hockey player. Not everyone is going to be a hockey player. They might do something else that they are successful at – God has a different plan for each one of us. You just have to work your hardest at whatever you're doing at the time, and the Lord makes it pretty clear when change is needed, or when you need to go in a different direction. If you just trust in the Lord and work hard at what you're doing, He'll always lead you on the right path."

"Show me your ways, O Lord, teach me your paths; guide me in your truth and teach me, for you are God my Savior, and my hope is in you all day long." Psalm 25:4-5

B.J. Crombeen

Based on B.J.'s story and favorite scriptures, how might you answer these questions in reflecting on your own story?

1. What have been your experiences of living on your own? What kinds of challenges have you faced? How might B.J.'s experience help you?

2. What are your greatest challenges and frustrations? What realizations have you made in the midst of these challenges? Have you ever looked to the Bible to help you through these challenges? What did you find?

3. Do you have a chapel program in your league? Have you gone to chapel, or would you consider going to chapel? How might a chapel program help you?

4. What kinds of experiences have you had, that might have put on the brakes in your journey? How might B.J.'s story of how he handles his diabetes encourage you?

5. From where do you draw encouragement? Who is your support system and how do they help you to do the right things and stay on the right path?

6. What encouraged you most about B.J.'s story? What could you relate to the most, and how might some of his experiences and perspectives apply to your life?

Brandon James, July '87

Brandon enjoyed soccer

BJ was also a serious lacrosse player

Played lacrosse with Sarnia Pacers

Brandon, age 8 – Clearwater Minor Novice 1993

Played AAA with York Simcoe Express

B.J. with his wife, Janet

Shane Doan

Shane, 16 yrs – 1st yr WHL, Kamloops Blazers 1993

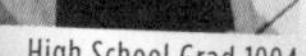

High School Grad 1994

1995 Memorial Cup Champs – Kamloops Blazers. Shane was MVP with Jarome Iginla

Strong and steady. *That pretty much sums up the man who grew up on a place called Circle Square Ranch in rural Halkirk, Alberta. He describes his early start as "the best childhood you could possibly have." His dad is his hero, and his parents gave him every advantage to play the sport he loved, enabling him to become the family man of faith he is today. "Strong and steady" is Shane Doan, in every aspect of his life, because sometimes, it's hard work to make the most of what you've been given.*

Growing up in Halkirk, population 120 or so, surrounded by prairies and farmland where the annual "Halkirk Bullarama" is held, it's a wonder that Shane didn't become a professional bull rider, instead of the NHL All-Star he is. You could say that hockey was in his blood, since his mom's brothers all played, and his dad had actually been drafted by the St. Louis Blues in his day. He also has a cousin or two who play the game at the highest level. A love of hockey isn't the only thing he inherited from his family, though. He had an incredible role model in his dad, who instilled in him a strong work ethic and biblical principles. "My dad was playing hockey, and he quit when he was twenty years old to go to Bible school. That's kind of my dad in a nutshell; it's all about principles for him. When he finished Bible school, he didn't know what he wanted to do, but he knew he wanted to help people. He was pretty good with his hands, so he helped to build a couple of homes. Then he got a call that my grandfather and my uncle donated some of the homestead land to Crossroads Christian Communications and they were building a camp. My dad wanted to do something with kids, so he said, 'Well, I can help build, I can work,' so he came home and said he'd be there for two years to help them build the camp – and he ended up being there for thirty-three years.

SHANE
DOAN – 19
Phoenix Coyotes

Right Wing | **Shoots: Right**
SIZE: 6'1" | WEIGHT: 210 LBS
BORN: OCTOBER 10, 1976
Halkirk, AB, Canada

Player Stats:

Selected 7th overall by the Winnipeg Jets in 1995 NHL Entry Draft

Won Memorial Cup and Stafford Smythe Memorial Trophy (MVP) with the Kamloops Blazers in 1995

Won 2 gold and 2 silver medals at IIHF world championships

Won World Cup of Hockey championship in 2004

Played in the NHL All Star game in 2004 and 2009

Was member of 2006 Canadian Olympic team

Won King Clancy Memorial Trophy in 2010

"Honestly, I've had the opportunity to play hockey in several different leagues and to meet some great men – very godly men – but my dad is the most godly man I know, because everything about him is truth. He wants to know the truth about life, the Bible, the scriptures, everything. He's an incredible man. You can't have a conversation with my dad for more than fifteen minutes before he brings up something about truth and principles and how you're going to live your life. That's what's on his heart, and so that's what comes out in every single conversation. He is such a good man, and he loves and cares more about me, my brother, my sister, and my mom than anything else. So, as a dad, that's what I want to exemplify."

Love of family is definitely a characteristic Shane's dad passed on to him. As a father of four himself now, his greatest delight is his family – from sitting in the stands watching his son, Josh, grow into his shoes, or, more appropriately, skates – to just hanging out at home and relaxing. Shane truly enjoys his family, and shows them the same love and care he received from his parents. "As much as I've been blessed in hockey, God has given me the most amazing wife that I could ever ask for. And because I have an amazing wife, I have an amazing mother for my kids, and they are a treat to be around. It's such a blast to be with them. They are truly, simply a gift from God."

Right behind his family, Shane takes seriously his role as captain of the Phoenix Coyotes, to be the biggest supporter and encourager to his teammates as he can be. He approaches his responsibility with humility and clarity of vision. "To be the captain is a huge honor. You look at the other players who have been captains and are captains now in the NHL, and I'm honored to be part of that group. I'm very grateful for the opportunity, and to the Coyotes for giving it to me. As captain, my job is to be the biggest cheerleader of the team. It's the coaches' job to critique and point out mistakes, but my job is to make sure everyone knows that they're vital and important. When people feel important, they want to contribute and do their best. I think for the most part, everyone who's playing a team sport is trying their best. Athletes just want to help their team win. They care more about that than anything else. So as captain, I have to make sure everyone knows they're important and that we need them to win. And I think that's what's made our team successful over the last couple of years. We use every single guy; it's not like we have one single superstar. We have twenty guys we count on every night, so I think it's so much more important in our organization that we have everyone working together."

Shane also goes above and beyond for his team, taking on personal responsibility for leading the team chapels, which is unusual for players, especially in the NHL. "That's something I've really enjoyed – that's fun. The guys know that I care about them and more as people than hockey players. I obviously want to win – I don't think anyone on my team would question my desire to win or my competitiveness. But they also know I care about them and want them to experience life, and the best life they can possibly have. I truly believe that Jesus came to give us life, and to give it even more abundantly than we could ever imagine, so our chapels are a way to try to help people understand that that's what I want for them. The only way anyone could understand how important that is to me is by having a relationship with me. People will listen to you when they know you care about them. Guys will come in and be totally themselves, and we'll have some full-on discussions because they want to know what's going on. And I want them to be as comfortable as possible because they know me and they know we can talk about anything."

Shane came by his strength and conviction of faith not only through his upbringing, but also by admitting he made plenty of mistakes. For Shane, being honest about not being perfect led to a stronger relationship with God. "I think everybody goes through trials and makes lots of mistakes. When I got to the NHL, I made mistakes, and I did things that were not necessarily the wisest. But you deal with your mistakes and you deal with the consequences, and that's when, for me personally, my faith was tested. Would it really be enough to sustain me if I admitted my mistakes and faced up to them?

How Does He Do That?
Shane's Special Training Tips

Do you have any special routines or training tips?

Shane: I run with a bunch of young guys, 17 to 25 year olds. All summer long, I run with these guys, and when we're done with our sprints and our cardio, we play a sport – football, soccer, ultimate Frisbee. I want to play a sport that gets my heart rate up, and that's something I think is vital because each sport allows you to work on different sets of skills.

One sport I specifically want my son to play is baseball because I think it teaches you to anticipate. So, if you're playing short and the ball gets hit to you and there's a runner on second, you can't just throw it to first. You have to hold the runner in check and make your play to first. In hockey, you have to have the ability to anticipate and to read the play. In baseball, it's part of the fundamentals. In our sport, it's something coaches look for, so I think baseball helps develop that ability. But playing every sport is vital and important.

And if you want to have good groins in hockey, you need to ride horses. The groin issue is a big thing in hockey because everyone hurts their groin in the motion of skating. I haven't had any problems with my groin, and I totally attribute that to riding horses.

"I wanted people to perceive me as being like my dad, and I am not like my dad in so many ways. I don't know if my dad's ever made a mistake in his life. So it was hard, and at times I felt like I was being a little fake, just trying to show people what I wanted them to see. I honestly wanted to be Christ-like, and I didn't ever want anyone to think I'd ever made a mistake. What I learned was that you have to be real. Now I have a much better understanding of who I am. God made me different than He made my dad, and I'm to be comfortable in who I am, and confident in that because that's how He made me, and He has His own purpose for me.

Training for Life with Shane Doan:
A favorite verse

Romans 8:28: *"And we know that in all things God works for the good of those who love him, who have been called according to his purpose."*

"I feel bad for the Christian kids who think, 'I can't make a mistake, and if I do, I have to hide it from my parents, or hide it from the people who are counting on me. From making mistakes, you get humbled, and you can't express enough how amazing God's grace is. I really think that, too often, as an athlete who becomes well-known, you get put up on a pedestal, and if it becomes known that you're a Christian athlete, you often get put up on an even higher pedestal. And by all means, we are to shine our light and not hide from that, but when we make a mistake, we should man up to it and not keep any secrets. Secrets are the worst thing that you can possibly have. Secrets are what destroy people time and time again. If you can simply acknowledge your mistakes and deal with them up front and not hide them, that's the type of man you're going to be able to live with, and the type of men we need.

"**As a Christian**, one of the things I think is so important and I think gets missed so much is that you have to have a genuine relationship with God. Young Christian men can be so zealous at times. At sixteen or eighteen years old, they're going away from home for the first time, and if they try to put up a false bravado of who they are as a Christian by always talking about 'I don't do this, and I don't do that,' they're setting themselves up for some hard times. If you're genuine, you cannot fake it. When you can have a genuine relationship with God, you will be so much more genuine and so much more respected by other people around you.

"**Just look at Peter, a disciple of Jesus**, and David, who was the man after God's own heart. I love Peter and David because even though they were chosen by God, they both made huge mistakes! But they faced them and they dealt with them honestly, and that's what we need to do as Christians too. Sometimes, we think, 'I don't want anyone to know what I'm really like, because if they know what I'm really like, they're going to realize I'm not this great person they thought I was.' And yet, God made you just the way He wants you, and He's not done with you. He understands. He knew you were going to make those mistakes a long time ago. He just wants no secrets. Being a Christian doesn't mean you're not a sinner. It means you understand the fact that you've sinned. But if you hide those things, it's going to eventually catch up to you."

Shane also realizes how easy it is to be misunderstood as a Christian in the hockey world. "Hockey is an intense emotional game, and I'm not afraid to play physical. I enjoy playing physical and the combativeness of it. I can get really emotional in a game. And sometimes people may not understand this. They would come up to me and ask, 'well, what happened there, why were you acting like that, why are you doing this?' And yet, to my teammates, that's what they wanted me to be. It might look like anger to people who don't understand the game, but it's not. It's more competitiveness to me. I've been in fights with my friends because that's part of our game, that's part of what we do. For a long time, Christianity wasn't necessarily viewed as a strength in hockey, so I think it's important for me to help people understand that, as a Christian, everything I do, I do with all my heart, as working for the Lord, not for men. So if you're going to compete against me, I'm going to compete so hard, because I want to win, and I do it as unto the Lord. And in doing that, my teammates also respect me more."

Training for Life with Shane Doan:
A favorite verse

Proverbs 10:4: *"Lazy hands make a man poor, but diligent hands bring wealth."* When I first broke into the League, I wrote Proverbs 10:4 on my sticks. You talk about your hands all the time in hockey, and I always thought I'd better not have lazy hands.

Shane's faith is the driving force in his ability to stay strong and steady, on the ice and off. His passion drives him to be the best player, and to encourage others to be the best they can be, at whatever they choose to do. "The reason I think that Christianity makes me better as a player is the passion and the intensity I have. That is what the Lord was talking about when He said, 'I came to give you life, and give it more fully' (John 10:10). For a long time, I thought, 'Well, I have to make sure I talk right and I do right because God's watching,' and I think I was missing the point that, no, it means that when I play hockey, I play it as hard as I can because that is what God has for me to do.

"I love horses, I raise horses, and you cannot imagine the passion and intensity of our studs when they're out. Before you turn them into the herd, they are the most well-mannered, quiet horses. I could put my kids on them, and they're amazing with them. But when you put them in a herd, and you watch them in their prime, and when you see a stallion that is fully in control of his herd and the intensity that is in these animals, it's amazing to think that God created that. That intensity is what I want all the time. I even tell my kids, 'I want you guys to do everything in life unto the Lord. If it's singing a song, then sing it! Don't be a wallflower and sit on the sidelines. Do your best in everything you do.' If you're around someone whose enthusiasm is being guided by God, it is so contagious. People can't help wanting to be around that person. Growing up on the ranch, we had camp counselors who were like that. They did everything as unto the Lord. If it was face painting, they'd paint their faces to the point where it looked amazing. It would be intense, or it would be hilarious, or it would be extreme. Those were the people you wanted to be around. If it's guided by God, that's what He's talking about when He says, 'Do it heartily,' and that's why I think it helps my hockey."

Shane's work ethic of "working heartily" is seen in the accomplishments and high times of his career, such as being named to the Memorial Cup All-Star team, winning the Stafford Smythe Memorial Trophy, playing in two NHL All-Star games, and winning the King Clancy Memorial Trophy, to name a few. His work ethic can also be seen in how he handles the low times. Again, strong and steady. "One of the high points was playing in the 2009 NHL playoffs. The team was picked to finish last in the whole NHL by everybody, and we ended up having the fourth most points and making the playoffs, really surprising everyone. It was incredible. The low point was probably in that exact same time. I had waited for so long for an opportunity to play in the playoffs, and I was so hungry to play and had so much passion to play in the playoffs and to be part of something like that. Then I separated my shoulder in game three and wasn't able to finish the playoffs. I waited seven years to make the playoffs, battling with a team that had fought and struggled to get there and no one expected to make it. Then finally to have the success as a team, only to get hurt in a game and not be able to finish, was one of the lows for sure."

This sounds very similar to an earlier time, when Shane was seventeen, in the WHL, and had almost the same experience. "My team, the Kamloops Blazers, made it to the Memorial Cup, and I blew out my knee. They went on to win the Cup, and I had to sit out. In fact, I sat out for ten months. When that happened, that was something I was very disappointed in and it really bothered me for quite a while. I didn't understand, and I started to question everything. I wondered why God let this happen to me. How could this happen now, before my career even got started? As it turned out, I came back the next year and had a good year, and was able to go on from there and get drafted. But at the time, I really just thought it wasn't fair.

"One thing we can get caught up in doing is keeping track of what happens in our lives and thinking, 'Well, I've got two unfair things against me now – that's really unfair!' But what I understand is that life isn't going to be fair all the time. In fact, I've been far more blessed than some people, and *that's* not fair! Others have worked hard and done the right things, and it hasn't worked out as well for them. But you know what else isn't fair? Grace! We get to go to Heaven because of what Jesus did – and that's not fair, but that's why it's called *grace*. The incredible story of the Gospel is we do not get what we deserve. We receive God's grace through Christ."

Shane would also experience grace in the face of another low point in his career – possibly one of the most unfair circumstances a person can experience. Not in the pain and regret of an injury this time, but in the sting of false accusation.

The accusation? Racial slurs expressed toward four francophone hockey officials in a game against the Montreal Canadiens on December 13, 2005. The facts? Shane did not utter any such slurs, and he was cleared of any wrong-doing through a comprehensive NHL investigation. Unfortunately, this controversy couldn't have come at a worse time. Shane had been selected for the 2006 Olympics Canadian national men's hockey team, which was a dream he had had since he was a kid. "It was the most frustrating thing, because in my whole life, I wanted to play for Team Canada in the Olympics. I'm the biggest Olympic fan there is, I love the Olympics – it's so much bigger than sports, just the whole spirit of it. So when I got selected to be on the Olympic team, and then those accusations came out, it really ruined my moment of being excited to talk to my family and share the excitement of being on the Olympic team. Instead, I was having to defend myself over something that was completely false, which was mind-blowing to me and bothered me quite a bit.

Training for Life with Shane Doan:
A favorite verse

Proverbs: I would read the Proverb for the day of the week – for example, Proverbs 17 on the 17th, etc. This was a good discipline for me.

"**The hardest part was settling it in my spirit.** Romans 8:28 says, 'And we know that in all things God works for the good of those who love him, who have been called according to his purpose,' and I was thinking, 'What good is possibly going to come out of this?' All I could say was that I never said that, but anytime I said something to defend myself, it just seemed to work against me. In my spirit, I knew I hadn't done anything wrong, and I never once tried to hide from anything. It was just very frustrating to deal with that, to have my name slandered, and my mom and dad's name. I have a very strong family, and they were even getting heat. They were sending reporters to my grandmother's house. It was unbelievable.

"But yet, in the end, the whole country of Canada seemed to be supporting me. A lot of the players I've played with, players I've played against, and fans who posted comments online. Even the Prime Minister of Canada eventually called me, and Hockey Canada was great. They stood up for me and defended me, and I thank God He had the right people in place who were capable to do that. And when the truth finally came out, everything was fine. Then I could see that something that was supposed to be a negative eventually turned into a positive, even though, in the middle of it, I couldn't believe what was going on. When the whole thing started to turn in our favor, I could see how all things do work for good, even though it didn't make sense to me at the time.

"**That was one of the hardest things I've been through.** All I wanted was for (the person who filed the suit) to say, 'I never met Shane, and I never knew him, but now that I've talked with him, I know he never would have said that.' That never happened, but it did come out that I didn't say what I was accused of saying. And yet, it just goes to show that you don't have that much control over your life, so you'd better acknowledge that God is in control. As much as you want to think you have control, it can turn and get away from you so fast, so you'd better stay humble."

Not only was Shane cleared of the allegations against him, he was promoted to team captain at the 2007 World Championships in Moscow, which prompted a demand from the Canadian Official Languages parliamentary committee for Hockey Canada to explain their decision. But the decision was maintained. Amusingly, a little bit of justification followed.

"We were in Russia when they started to come after me about this issue again – and the next game, I scored a hat trick. It was kind of funny because the joke was that I hadn't scored a hat trick in my professional career, and I got one the next day at the World Championships. It felt kind of like God was saying, 'I'll take care of this. You just do your job.' I don't normally think like that, but that's how it felt at the time." Not only did Shane score a hat trick within six minutes 25 seconds which led to a victory over Belarus in the qualification round, but he also scored the game winning goal in the victorious preliminary round against Norway, and Team Canada ended up going undefeated against Finland in the finals to win the gold medal. Not that Shane sees a direct cause-and-effect, but it does make for a great story in light of everything he has gone through.

"I don't want that incident to be something I'm remembered for. I just want to show people who I really am, and that I care. I think the fact that I'm a Christian helped me significantly because people know that I'm real in what I believe – and because of that, it was very rewarding that they were saying, 'If he said he didn't say that, he didn't say it.' And having that support and people defending me like that is not something I take lightly. So now, when it comes up, it's settled and it's done."

Most likely, being a strong and steady player who cares about people is what Shane Doan will be best known for. As a team captain, he cares about forming relationships with his teammates and pouring himself into their lives. Even when they leave the team, Shane maintains his relationships and has nothing but respect for the players he's come to call friends, whether they're on the same side of the ice, or across it. "The guys I played with in Juniors and now play in the NHL – guys like Jarome Iginla and Jason Strudwick and Darcy Tucker, and all these different guys – I've played against them, and we're all really good friends. When you play against each other, you're going for bragging rights. I want to beat those guys as bad or worse than anyone else! It just comes back to how close everyone is."

Training for Life with Shane Doan: A favorite verse

Jeremiah 29:11: *"For I know the plans I have for you," declares the Lord, "plans to prosper you and not to harm you, plans to give you hope and a future."*

There's a story behind Romans 8:28 and Jeremiah 29:11. I got sent down to the minors in my third year in the League. I'd had a great training camp, and I'd led the team in scoring in exhibition – then kind of out of nowhere, I got sent down. It was my 159th game, and I didn't realize at the time it was because of my contract. So they sent me down, even though I was having my best training camp and I was doing well. I was just getting to the point where I was really able to contribute, and when they sent me down, I thought, "What? This isn't fair! How could they do this to me?" And so I went down and pouted for the first nine games in the minors, and then after I'd been there for about nine or ten games, I stopped feeling sorry for myself and started playing again – and that's when those scriptures really came in. Knowing God has a plan for me, to give me hope and a future helped me not to get caught up in what was going on at the moment. Some good things also happened during that time. I had a blast with the group of guys that were there. On top of that, my cousin was playing in the city next door, so we got to hang out with him and his wife, and they became good friends of ours.

I use that experience sometimes to encourage guys who are going through the same kind of thing. I am the first one to tell guys I had 22 goals in four years of playing. I scored 7 goals my first year, 4 my second, 5 my third, and 6 my fourth. Some guys will get up to the NHL and not have the success they want, and they'll start thinking, "What's wrong with me? I can't believe this!" I just tell them to have faith that they're a good player, and it will eventually work out. It is such a mind game, and there is such a small gap between players who are good and players who don't make it. It's so much in your head – it's that confidence in who you are that you can't let anyone shake.

Hockey is unique in that guys can be traded pretty much anytime, up to a certain point in the season, with or without warning. That means that a player could show up for practice one day, get sent off to some other team, and by that night, even play in a game against the guys who were teammates just hours before. As captain, Shane not only finds himself saying goodbye to friends he's poured his heart and soul into, but also helping new teammates adjust quickly and building solidarity within the team. It's a part of the sport, but it isn't always easy to manage. Hearing Shane talk about it just reinforces how much he cares about people. "Dealing with that is probably one of the hardest things in all of hockey. One of the guys I always think of is Teppo Numminen. He and I played together, and he is one of the guys I admire and respect as much as anyone I've played with. He's someone who I saw and spent time with day to day for ten years of my life, then he was traded to Dallas, and all of a sudden, we hardly see each other anymore. It's one of the things in the business you just accept, and you wish it wasn't the way it is, but it is.

"With the Coyotes, it's about keeping solidarity of spirit on the team. The last few years here have been a challenge, in that we've had every excuse to just fold it up, pack in the tents and say, 'OK, we're done. We don't have a chance. We don't have an owner,' and talk about what we don't have. But we have a great group of guys here, and as I said before, I think it's because we count on every single guy every night, and we work together. We stick with it and just stay true to our identity as a team."

"**Staying true" is a constant theme in Shane's journey.** After all, it's that foundation of truth instilled in him as a kid, honed through experience, and sharpened through challenges and trials that has made him the strong and steady husband, dad, son, brother, friend, teammate, captain, and all-star he is today. It's a message he's passionate about, whether he's talking with his kids, his team or rising young Christian athletes.

"**If there's one thing I would stress beyond anything** to young Christian athletes is just to be real. Don't try to think you have to be more or less than the person God made you to be. I see some kids who are Christians, and they're incredible speakers, and I think some young Christian athletes want to think, 'Because I'm an athlete, and because I have this pulpit, I have to do that too.' You be real, and in being real, you'll be the person God made you to be and not worry about trying to be someone you think you're supposed to be. Be the man or woman God wants you to be, and don't be superficial with your relationship with God. Be real. If you're an eagle, be an eagle. But if you're a gopher, be the best gopher you can be. I think too often Christian athletes think that because we have a pedestal, we're supposed to be bigger than who we are. It's easy to assume that if you're successful in one area, then you'll be successful in everything. Be OK with saying,

'I'm not that, I'm good at this. Let me be the best I can be at this.' And God will take care of the rest."

"Have I not commanded you? Be strong and courageous... Do not be discouraged, for the Lord your God will be with you wherever you go." Joshua 1:9

Shane Doan

Based on Shane's story and favorite scriptures, how might you answer these questions in reflecting on your own story?

1. What words would you use to sum up your story? Is this what you want to be remembered for? If so, how do you demonstrate these characteristics? If not, what would you change?
2. Have you ever felt like you weren't being true to yourself, or a little fake? How has Shane's story challenged you to be genuine?
3. Have you ever been tempted to hide your mistakes and keep them a secret? How did you feel about that? What was the result? What could you do differently?
4. How would you describe your relationship with the Lord? How has Shane's story challenged you to see Him at work in your life?
5. How could you apply Shane's perspective of doing everything as unto the Lord, to your hockey and your life, in good times and low times?
6. What encouraged you most about Shane's story? What could you relate to the most, and how might some of his experiences and perspectives apply to your life?

Shane, 7 or 8 yrs – Castor Beavers Novice

Castor 10 and unders – New Cooperalls, a gift from his Grandpa for 9th birthday

Shane, 14 yrs – Southern Alberta Selects played in Super Series with Ryan Smyth

Shane and Red Wing – no saddle, no bridle

Shane and Red Wing, 1995

Doan family with Johnny and June Cash, 1987

Mike Fisher

The Fisher Family (L to R) outside their home in Bridgenorth, (Mike, Meredith, Rob, Bud, Karen, Jim)

Meredith, Rob, and Mike (age 4) in their home in Bridgenorth

Mike as captain of "AAA" Minor Petes team

> "**Feb 10, 2011 OTTAWA** – *Ottawa Senators general manager Bryan Murray announced today the club has acquired a first-round draft pick in the 2011 entry draft and a third-round draft pick in 2012 from the Nashville Predators in exchange for forward Mike Fisher. Fisher, 30, who is in his 11th full season in the NHL, has played all 675 games of his career with the Senators..." [1]*

It happens all the time these days in the NHL. You show up to the rink for a regular practice, maybe preparing for a game that night, and the coach calls you over to deliver the news that you've been traded. Right now. Pack your things and head to a new city, a new team, in time for a different game tonight than the one you had on your mind. Knowing this could happen is vastly different from actually experiencing it, especially after 11 seasons and 675 games with the same team. How does one respond to news like that? What do you say to your teammates – guys you've grown to know and with whom you've formed a bond that can only be forged through riding the wave of highs and lows of competition and battle, who have now instantly become "the opposition?" And what do you say to the thousands of fans who have poured out their love and devotion game after game?

If you're Mike Fisher, yes, you may be caught a bit off guard and have the expected swirl of emotions go through your mind, but then you act with the integrity and class that have come to define your character and career. As an example, Mike did not complete the quick journey from Ottawa to Nashville without first taking out a full-page ad in the *Ottawa Citizen*, thanking Ottawa, the Senators, and the fans for supporting him throughout his career. In addition, when asked about what kind of legacy he wanted to leave behind in Ottawa, he could have said he wanted to be remembered for his 181 goals, 195 assists, and 620 penalty minutes with the Sens, but, instead, he quietly said, "I think it would have to be that I had a heart for people and helping others. To me, just showing Christ's love to others in whatever way we can is a success." Maybe not exactly what you'd expect to hear. But then again, given his upbringing and outspoken commitment to his faith, not a big surprise either.

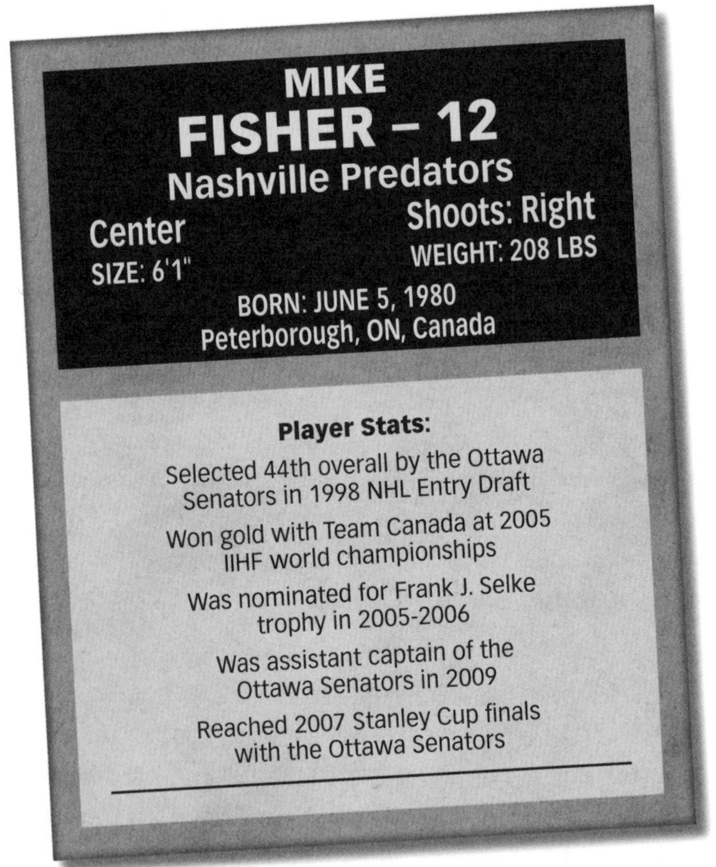

Mike's story of faith and hockey began in Peterborough, Ontario, where his parents instilled in him, his two brothers, and sister the importance of putting God first and demonstrating what it was like to be a follower of Jesus Christ. "My parents are both strong Christian people, and great godly influences on me. I remember, after meals, we'd have a little Bible study, or they'd read a little devotional – maybe five or ten minutes. We didn't always enjoy that as little kids. I wanted to get outside and play hockey, but they wanted to make a point. Dinner time was a big thing, and even though we were busy, just to have a quick study and prayer really stressed to me that a relationship with the Lord had to be ahead of hockey." This was a principle Mike's parents were fully committed to, even with the demands of a sport like hockey, they found substantive ways to live it out. "Sometimes I would miss certain things. I remember missing some Sunday morning practices so we could go to church. Obviously, at a certain point, you can't be missing tournaments and things like that, if you want to continue on and get serious about hockey. But it was all about having a strong relationship with the Lord, making sure you're doing the right things, and making sure your heart is right. You have to find a balance in that."

Training for Life with Mike Fisher: A favorite verse

Proverbs 3:5-6: "Trust in the Lord with all your heart and lean not on your own understanding; in all your ways acknowledge him, and he will make your paths straight." To me, when I'm going through a situation I really don't understand and I'm not sure what's going on, this is a good verse to remind me that it's not about my understanding. I can just do what I can do, and trust in Him to see me through. This is a comforting verse too, and one I pass on most to friends and other people.

That balance also included keeping realistic expectations where hockey was concerned. "As far as hockey was concerned, they always let me make my own decisions. They never pressured me to do anything, but always said that they would support whatever I wanted to do with hockey. That support just allowed me to relax and have fun and realize that you're either born with the desire and the ability and the work ethic or you're not. You can't force kids or pressure them. You can help them with those things, but you've got to have it in the first place, or it isn't going to do a kid any good. It has to be fun."

How Does He Do That? Mike's Special Training Tips

Do you have any tips, or special things you do to make you the player you are?

Mike: Off-ice training is big – preparing in the summer and getting your body ready is really important. I've also started working with a skating coach. I think this really helps – just working one-on-one on skating, edge work, and different skill drills. Some guys do scrimmaging in the summer, but I think you can develop bad habits, and the workout isn't very intense, so I get more out of just working hard on my skating.

Also, shooting a lot of pucks is good practice. Through the years, I've worked on my shot a lot – in the basement as a kid, then I have this net that goes over the garage door. It's the size of a garage door and comes down over it when you put the door up, and I shoot pucks into it. There's a lot of little stuff you can do. It doesn't matter where you are, you can still work on the little parts of your game.

"Fun" may well have described Mike's first few years leading up to and playing professional hockey, leaving home for the first time at the age of 17 to play in the Ontario Hockey League for the Sudbury Wolves. Then just two short years later, he was drafted in the second round by the NHL's Ottawa Senators. Early success and the desire to fit in with teammates and slide into an NHL lifestyle took its toll on his faith journey, however. "At 19 in Ottawa, I was away from home for a long time. I struggled in my faith. Growing up, I always wanted to play in the NHL. That was a huge goal. When I became a teenager, it became more of an obsession. Certain things, like my walk with the Lord started to fade a little bit. I think as time went on, I started to fall away from the Lord. I got to the NHL at age 19, realized my dream, and it was exciting. But at the same time, I think I got caught up in making money and all the things that come along with the game at a young age, and that kind of took over. Like the prodigal son who went away for a little bit, I tested the waters and wanted to see what the real world was like."

Not an uncommon experience for most young people leaving home for the first time, but most young people are not thrown so quickly into a lifestyle of fame and fortune. "Like my dad always said, 'it takes a steady hand to hold a full plate,' and you get a full plate pretty early." It might have been his fast track to success, or the realization that maybe his hand wasn't so steady, that caused Mike to re-examine his life and his priorities. "It took about two years, and I just wasn't happy with a lot of things. I realized there was so much more, and that I wasn't using the talents and abilities that God had given me in the right ways, and I wasn't sharing or living the way I knew God wanted me to live, in following Him. Growing up in a Christian family, I knew I wasn't living right. I knew I really believed in everything I'd been taught as a kid, but I needed to find out if it was real for me."

Everyone experiences key decision points that can determine the trajectory of the rest of their life. For Mike, the decision to return to the faith of his youth took some time. It began with a realization that he wasn't the man he wanted to be. "I knew who I wanted to be, and I made some bad decisions that I knew were all wrong. It's so easy to get caught up in what everyone else is doing. Sometimes, it takes some struggles or a battle, and then you figure it out. Sometimes, you need to go away, but when you come back you appreciate everything so much more."

Realization is a great place to start, but realization without action doesn't lead to real change. Action, though, takes courage, determination, and discipline – qualities that have been definitive of Mike's character, honed throughout his journey. "It took a bit of time. Slowly, I got back into the Word, reading and praying, and slowly coming back to the Lord. When I left for the NHL, I tried to be a Christian kid, and told myself I wasn't going to drink or do all of these things Christians aren't supposed to do. But I think I was trying too hard under my own power, not under the Lord's power. Instead of finding strength in His Word and through prayer, I tried to turn things around in my own strength, and when we do that, we're most likely going to fail. I realized that and started getting into the Word and having a hunger and getting a taste of what it's really like to follow Christ. I finally really got that for the first time when I was 21 or 22. I thought, 'this is awesome, there's no other way.' I just grew up. There wasn't any "ah ha" moment. It was a gradual heart change, a period of praying and people praying for me, but it happened."

"**One of the scriptures that hit home** for me and was a big part of the change in me was Luke 9:23-25, "If anyone would come after me, he must deny himself and take up his cross daily and follow me..." Then it gets awesome, "...What good is it for a man to gain the whole world, and yet lose or forfeit his very self?" And I remember feeling like, man, here I've gained the whole world, living my dream, but I feel like I'm losing my soul in the process, and that needed to be changed. I needed some time to regroup, apart from the guilt and the shame, because that stuff will eat you up, but it's hard to get out of that. Fortunately, I had a lot of good people around me."

Training for Life with Mike Fisher: A favorite verse

Romans 12:12: "Be joyful in hope, patient in affliction, faithful in prayer." This is a simple scripture, but a good reminder to me, and one I put on my sticks. There's also a story behind this one. During the 2005-2006 season, I was having a good year, but I injured my knee at the end of December. We were hoping to make the playoffs, and I was worried that I'd miss it all. As I was helped into the dressing room, I looked at the clock, and it was stopped at 12:12. I remember I was just struck by that reminder that God is in control, and it really helped me to relax and to trust Him.

The people in Mike's life have certainly played a key role in his journey. From the example set for him by his parents, to friends and family members who form a strong support group around him. He says, "Friends make you stronger, and help make you who you are." One of his closest friends is his cousin, Warren, who he describes as his spiritual mentor. "My parents were obviously praying for me during this time, and my biggest supporter was my cousin. He was with me all the time, through prayer and study, and throughout those times, he was a big influence for sure. He was solid. He's been through a lot of the same things I had, and he could really relate. I believe God put him there for a reason, for just the right time."

Training for Life with Mike Fisher: A favorite verse

Luke 9:23-25: "Then he said to them all: "If anyone would come after me, he must deny himself and take up his cross daily and follow me. For whoever wants to save his life will lose it, but whoever loses his life for me will save it. What good is it for a man to gain the whole world, and yet lose or forfeit his very self?" I love this one. I remember going through it with my cousin in our study, and the thought of dying to yourself just kind of hit me. Like I was talking about earlier, this verse was definitely a life-changer. It's a constant reminder that following Christ is a daily thing, not just a one-time thing.

God put another person in Mike's life at just the right time – his wife, country music star, Carrie Underwood. Much has been published about their high-profile courtship and marriage, which Hollywood loves to exploit for selling magazines and creating "buzz". But for Mike and Carrie, theirs is a love story that is deeply personal and faith-filled. "The summer before I met Carrie, I was kind of ready. I trusted that the Lord would bring along the right one, and maybe I was at that point where I was a bit lonely. I don't know, but I was just ready, and I prayed that God would bring the right one. Then I met Carrie, and the more I got to know her, I could see that we're very similar in our stories. With everything she's gone through – becoming famous in a matter of months and dealing with the pressures of that – I think right away we could relate, and that was exciting. For both of us, it was important that we found someone who shared the same faith and values, who was your best friend, and knowing pretty early this is someone you could share a life with and grow old with. Even early on, when she was touring and I was playing, and we weren't together a whole lot, we still did long distance Bible studies and prayed together, which we continue to do today. We both knew we needed our faith to be a huge part of our relationship if we were moving toward marriage. We just wanted to grow together spiritually, and that's why I think our relationship is so much stronger. It's true that the closer you get to God, the closer you're going to feel toward your spouse."

"We're pretty much just a normal couple. We don't go out in the spotlight and all those things. It is a different dynamic being married to someone of a higher profile than myself, but when we're relying on each other and praying through situations, that's what marriage is all about. When you've got someone who can help you along, and you can help each other, it's so much easier to go through different things and deal with some of life's pressures." Not so "normal" may have been their decision to go against the increasingly fast flow of what the culture defines as acceptable, and even expected. The rewards of this decision have exceeded their wildest imaginations. As Mike explains, "We decided early on that in our relationship, we were not going to have sex before marriage. We both had made mistakes along the way, and that's something we decided we weren't going to do. I don't mind saying, it was the hardest thing to do, but the Lord helped us through it, and we waited until we were married. We didn't even realize what that decision would do for us, but it made all the difference in getting to know each other, getting to know her heart, her beliefs, her faith, outside of the physical things. That was huge for us. But it has to be a goal. It's hard, but also brings you closer together when you know you're in it together, and you're relying on God's strength and asking Him to help you, and He will, and He did."

Mike is hopeful his parents' legacy of faith and love will continue in him and his own family. "They've given me a good sense of loving others. I've learned a lot from them, from their relationship, getting into the Word and the scriptures that I grew up seeing, and then the way they loved each other. And now being married, I see the importance of being surrounded by that and the way they loved us kids. I had a dad who loved me like no other. He would do anything for me, and that's helped me get a little taste of what God's love is like too. I'm grateful for that, and knowing God's love is so much greater than that. Trying to do that and create a home that's Christ-centered and serving others and growing together spiritually and having that rub off on our kids is exactly what my parents did, and we want to do. That's the dad I want to be and the husband I want to be. I've got some work to do for sure, but just seeing the way my dad loved my mom – I mean, if I can love like that, I'll be doing great!"

Love and service and…hockey? Well, why not – especially when these are the hallmarks of one of the toughest, most respected players in the game. Mike Fisher's parents led the way, providing a firm foundation of love and service, modeling the Christian life for their children, which is now bearing fruit in the next generation of Fishers. "I used to get up every morning, and my mom would have her Bible out and would be doing a study of some kind. She would always spend so much time in prayer, and in the Word. My dad would do anything for anyone. He showed his love more by just doing things and serving others. He never stops going." These generational traits are exhibited now by Mike, as he and Carrie look for ways to serve in their community. Mike is known for his community service in Ottawa, with Rogers House, a pediatric palliative care center for children in the Children's Hospital of Eastern Ontario, the Make-A-Wish Foundation, Hockey Ministries International, the Mike Fisher Hockey Camp, and the Mike Fisher Foundation, which is focused on helping the less fortunate. Mike has made his off-ice commitment clear – to serve wherever he finds a need that he is capable of meeting. Various Ottawa journals are full of stories of Mike's quiet service to the community, and most importantly, its people – resulting in the most common farewell sentiments from fans, singing the same chorus of, "We're going to greatly miss watching you play in a Senators uniform, but we'll miss your generosity and big heart even more." Wherever Mike goes, it won't change his missional focus: "My goal here is to find some needs and get involved. I see us being philanthropists and raising money in the ministry. That's what I see myself doing long-term."

Oh, and by the way, at the same time, Mike has some hockey to play! Changing teams may mean making adjustments and taking on a different role, but he was excited and ready for the fresh start and new opportunities. "Looking back on it now, I'm obviously very thankful that, if I was going to be traded, it was to Nashville, where I would be with Carrie. God's Hand was in that, there's no question. Just before I got traded, we were at the worst point in years. The team was really struggling, and we lost eleven games in a row. I wasn't playing that great, and no one was having fun at the rink. We expected better of ourselves and we had a good team, so it was very frustrating." After a rocky start following his trade to the Nashville Predators, Mike rallied to finish the end of the season with 12 points, and a respectable 7 points in 12 playoff games. Asked about the effect of the trade on his role, he reflected, "I was an assistant captain in Ottawa, then I got traded, and in a way you just want to fit in and get adjusted to the style of play, and get to know the guys. They hadn't had that much playoff experience, so that may have been one of the reasons they brought me here. That being said, I was trying to fit in, and felt a little bit of pressure to perform. I went through a pretty big slump, probably the biggest in my career, for a couple of weeks when I came to Nashville. That was tough, but I made it through and had a pretty decent playoff run. It's weird, but when you get traded, you put a lot of pressure on yourself to be the best you can be. I'll tell you, my first game at home in Nashville felt like my first game in the NHL. I was so nervous! It was so strange, being that nervous, but it ultimately worked out, and I love it here. It's really good."

How Does He Do That? *Mike's Special Training Tips*

Do you have any advice for young players who want to have an edge over their competition?

Mike: I always go back to skating first. I started power skating before I ever played any competitive hockey, so when you work on your skating constantly and strengthen your power, your edges, your balance and mobility, that's where it all starts. I always say to focus on your skating, and next to that would be your puck skills and skill drills. Those are things you can even do in your basement or outside in your driveway. In the ten years I've been playing, the game feels like it's getting quicker. Guys are getting bigger and stronger and working out earlier – so your skating skills are huge as the game is getting quicker.

Mike's experience is probably one most players can relate to at one point or another. Whether leaving home at a young age, or unexpectedly going through a trade, change is often the only constant in the hockey journey. The key is knowing how to handle change and stay on course. "The biggest thing is staying in touch with your family and friends. When I was struggling, I didn't talk to people much, and I kind of got into my own bubble. But I think the biggest thing is staying grounded, get in your faith, realize that this is the plan God has for you, and just embrace that and be excited about it. Sometimes those changes are a little bit scary, but if you ultimately really understand that God is in control, and that He's with you the whole way, it makes it a lot easier. You don't always see it when you're going through it, but when you look back and realize He was always with you, that makes the changes and uncertainty much easier to handle."

Teams may change, and teammates may come and go, but two of the things that remain the same for Mike Fisher are his style of hockey and his faith. Some may wonder how he reconciles the two. Known for his tenacity and being a player who's tough to play against, what does he have to say about how his faith affects his game, and vice versa? "I think that making that decision to follow Christ can be hard, especially when you're young, and maybe some of the other guys don't understand why you'd choose to go to church over a hockey practice, but I'll tell you, it's worth the reward, that's for sure. Sometimes the right thing is rough and not the easiest thing to do, but in making those hard decisions, God will see you through, and I'm glad I lived through those things. I think at times, my faith pushed me to want to prove to my teammates who didn't understand that I can make it in hockey as a Christian, and live out my faith, and use it to help drive me. I mean, I grew up watching Christian players like Laurie Boschman and Mike Gartner. I would follow them and want to be like them. And now, I think that the way I play is to try to play as hard as I can within the boundaries of the game, and respect other players. I play as hard as I can for my team, and ultimately, I play for the Lord."

Because he's so well respected for his toughness on the ice and the genuineness of his faith, Mike has become a role model to many, passing along the inspiration and encouragement he found in the guys he looked up to as a kid. Even teammates and some of the younger players coming into the NHL have expressed the impact he's made on them, just by being who he is, working hard, and remaining true to his character. You only need to spend a little time around Mike, and you can't miss his humility, his heart for people, and the gift he has to bring out the best in everyone. "Really, in building a relationship, it doesn't happen overnight. It's just the little things, of just showing guys that you care about them, on ice and off, and just really loving them, just being there for them through different things."

That's the mark of a true role model. Mike doesn't have to try to impress anyone; others just want to follow him and be like him because they see that he's for real. "That's a huge compliment for me. If someone comes up to me and says, 'you're my greatest role model,' that for me is a greater compliment than saying, 'you're my favorite player,' because that obviously speaks to how they see my character and the things that matter. It's also a great responsibility, and it's definitely an honor that others look up to me. I think I feel a little bit inadequate at times, but knowing that others are watching keeps me accountable. Hearing those things encourages me to want to do more and more, and be the best role model that I can. Knowing you've impacted one or two people along the way – oh, man, that's what it's all about! I know that's why God has gifted me and given me these talents. I've probably missed opportunities along the way, but those I've had have really given me that hunger to want to be more, and to want to give more – give it my all."

Looking ahead, Mike is full of optimism for the future. With a new team, a new wife, and hopes for passing his faith on to a new generation someday, he can only express thankfulness and amazement for the course of his journey. "I think the older I get, the more I kind of comprehend how great the Lord's love is. Just understanding that and realizing how much He loves us. Sometimes we lose sight of that and start to go astray, but I think of open arms. Always open arms through everything – ups, downs, struggles, failures, all of that. He's just there with open arms all the time. That's how much He loves us."

At the ripe old age of 31, Mike Fisher is already living the legacy he said he wanted to leave in Ottawa – remember? "I think it would have to be that I had a heart for people and helping others. To me, just showing Christ's love to others in whatever way we can is a success." That's a unique perspective, in a culture that defines "success" as the next promotion, the number of goals, hits or saves, or winning the Cup – all exhilarating moments that will eventually fade. Mike's journey toward success will be a living heritage...in the people he loved and those he opened *his* arms to along the way.

"Be joyful in hope, patient in affliction, faithful in prayer. Share with God's people who are in need. Practice hospitality." (Romans 12:12-13)

Mike Fisher

Based on Mike's story and favorite scriptures, how might you answer these questions in reflecting on your own story?

1. Have you ever had your plans abruptly altered, like Mike's were when he was traded to Nashville? How did you handle this? What could you learn from Mike's response that would help you handle future unexpected changes?
2. What principles do you value more than hockey or sports? How do you demonstrate your commitment to these principles?
3. Have you ever drifted away from your values, or your roots? Are you going through this right now? How might Mike's story help you through these times? Have you ever thought of the Bible as a source of encouragement and direction?
4. Who are the people who help you most? How do they help you? Do they help you to grow in your faith?
5. Have you had opportunities to serve your community? What have these experiences meant to you?
6. What's the legacy you want to leave behind at the end of your career?
7. What encouraged you most about Mike's story? What could you relate to the most, and how might some of his experiences and perspectives apply to your life?

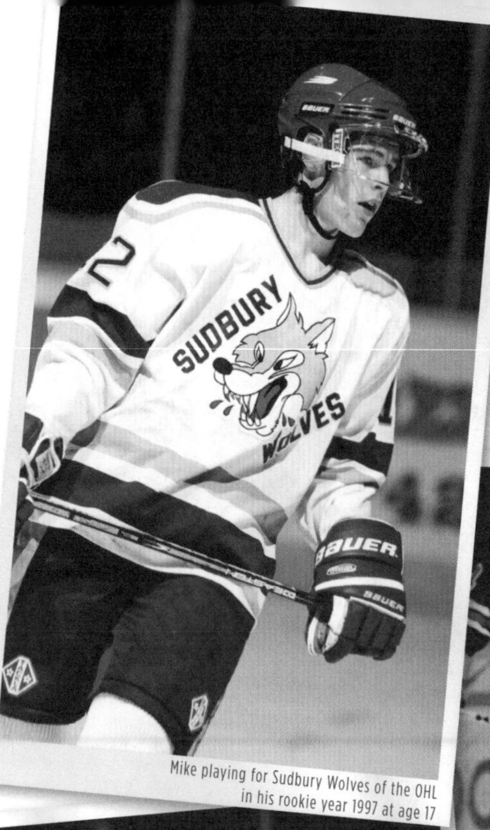

Mike playing for Sudbury Wolves of the OHL
in his rookie year 1997 at age 17

Mike playing tier 2 Jr. A for the Peterborough
"Bees" of the OHA at age 16

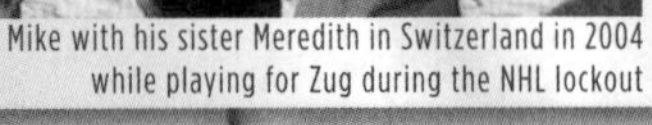

Mike with his sister Meredith in Switzerland in 2004
while playing for Zug during the NHL lockout

Mike in Switzerland in 2004

Mike with parents Jim & Karen at summit of Mt. Nieson in Switzerland in 2009
while playing for Team Cananda in the IIHF championships

BAUER
BAUER
Dan Hamhuis

Family Christmas photo at my Oma's house 1990

My second year of hockey age 5

Christmas morning 1991

How many people can say *that a broken leg at the age of 14 completely affected the course of their entire life? For most of us, a broken leg means a few weeks in a cast or on crutches – maybe missing an event or two – but when it's healed, life pretty much resumes on the same course it was on before. But for a young Dan Hamhuis, one of the best defensemen in British Columbia in his junior draft season, it meant missing the B.C. Winter Games – an annual showcase tournament – and, as a result, not being drafted into the Western Hockey League. While devastating at the time, little did Dan know that this incident would put into motion a theme in his life's journey of opportunities and blessings that would come as a result of injuries and disappointments. In this case, a broken leg led to a distinguished National Hockey League and International hockey career, as well as a wife and family – not exactly the typical results from a broken leg. But we're getting ahead of ourselves.*

For Dan Hamhuis, playing hockey was never really a decision. "My parents put me in hockey at four years old, and I don't remember much of those first few years, but I know I really liked it. I have memories of playing for hours on the outdoor rink in our backyard that my dad made for me, and playing with him in the basement. As I got a little bit older, 10 and 11 years old, I started to become one of the better players. I think I just became good because I enjoyed it so much and spent so many hours playing street hockey and doing extra things. When I was 13, 14, 15, playing in the NHL was a dream, but I never thought I would make it because I was from such a small town."

Dan's parents wanted to give him an advantage beyond an early start in hockey. "I grew up in a Christian home and went to a Christian school. I saw from my parents how important it was to go to church, and they taught me good values and instilled the truth in me." Dan would come to discover that exceptional skills, coupled with strong moral character, would serve him well, especially when he went away for the first time and found himself tested, both in hockey as well as his faith.

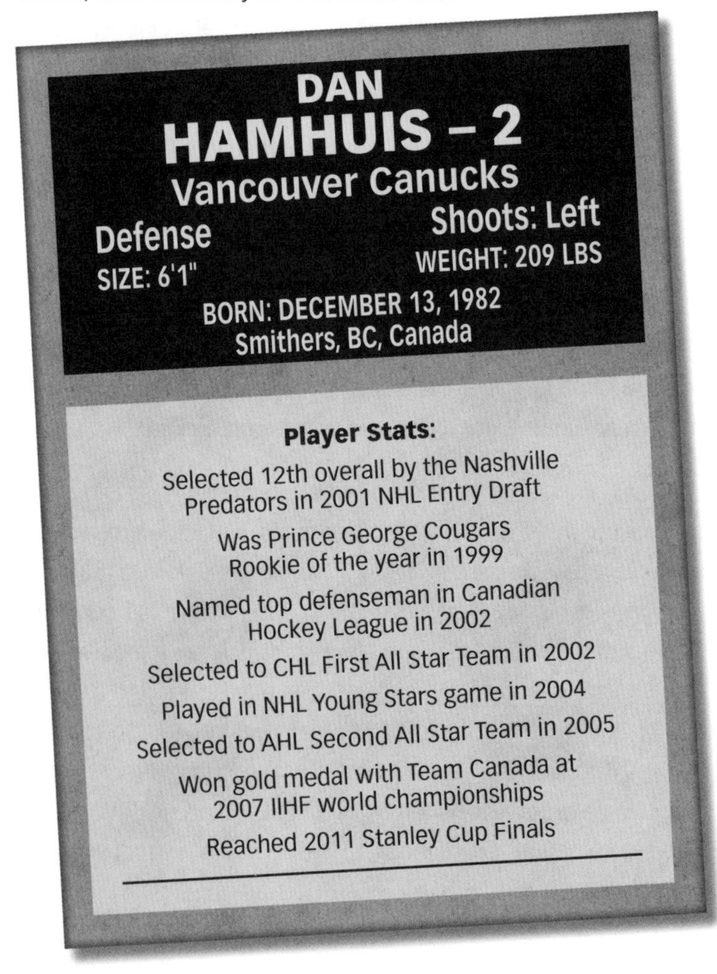

The season after missing the first WHL draft for which he was eligible (because of that broken leg), Dan played in a tournament in Prince George. "As it turned out, since I wasn't drafted, the Prince George Cougars invited me to their training camp, which was a great situation because it was the closest junior team to my home town. I made the team in Prince George and went on to play there for the next four years. While I was there, I was attending church fairly regularly, and guys on the team know that I was a Christian. I felt like I had the responsibility to be a good example to them. From 16 to 19 years old I was immature in my faith, but I had a strong conscience. I suppose God was there kind of telling me 'You're in a unique position being a Christian on this team.' That's kind of where it hit me, and I started to think about it more on my own. But I struggled with it. There are a lot of temptations in junior that are easy to fall for. Off the ice there are lots of things that could sidetrack a hockey career, like drinking, girls, and partying. This is easy to get caught up in, and I had to lean on my upbringing and faith to help me make some good decisions. Unfortunately, there were some guys along the way who got sidetracked, and it ruined some promising hockey careers. In junior, you're in a smaller town and can become quite popular, and that can be a bit of a challenge sometimes. Thinking you're more than you are and losing that humble, hard-working attitude can also sidetrack your hockey career and your life too. It can be very difficult at times, and that was a real battle for me to choose the right things. Sometimes I did, and sometimes I didn't. Certainly, for me, growing up in a Christian family, I was very aware when I was doing things I shouldn't have been doing. I think that was God talking and telling me that I might be making a wrong decision here, and I should be doing something different. I'm still very aware of that. When I do make the wrong decision, it's a terrible feeling. And when I make the right ones, it always feels way better that I made that decision, even though initially it may be more difficult. I think that's what guided me in my younger years, in junior.

How Does He Do That? Dan's Special Training Tips

Do you have any specific routines that help you to be the kind of player you are – any "inside tips?"

Dan: For the games, I'm not superstitious – I'd say I'm routine. I take a lot of time in my warn-up and preparation to be sure I'm ready to go. One thing that helps me in my hockey, and mentally, is thinking positively, no matter how I feel or what's led up to the game. When I step out onto the ice, I just believe it's going to be a good night. Even before, that afternoon, I'll try to do a little bit of visualization of the game and run positive images of things going well on the ice through my head. If I think of bad things happening, I try to re-run that in a good way, and that helped me a lot in this past year to be more consistent in the game.

"**A huge transition in my life**, and when my faith really hit home, was when I went to play my first year professional. I was drafted by Nashville in 2001, and after a couple of unsuccessful training camps, they sent me to the American Hockey League to play a season in Milwaukee. While Prince George had been comfortably close to home, and I was familiar with the city and close to my teammates, that first year in Milwaukee was a tough year for me. Even though it ended up being a huge turning point in my life and in my faith life, it was one of the worst years I've had in hockey. Coming from such a great junior hockey environment in Prince George to going to Milwaukee, where we played in a 17,000 seat arena with maybe 5,000 people in it, was an adjustment. Living on my own for the first time, being far away from family and friends, and playing with twenty new guys who were all older than me was really intimidating and a tough transition. It was a lonely time for me. I didn't play that well, and I had my struggles off the ice as well."

His time in Milwaukee, however, would represent the second time in his hockey career that Dan would experience a life-changing blessing as a result of difficult times. "We had a chaplain there named Iggy Cofaro with Hockey Ministries International, and he kind of shook me up a bit. We had a pretty big group of people going to chapel, and he challenged us, and I think me in particular, that growing up knowing about God is not good enough. He painted a vivid picture of Jesus' love for us through the sacrifice he made dying on the cross. This motivated and inspired me to live the way Jesus taught and demonstrated for us. I think Iggy knew that I needed this at this point in my faith journey. I was actually kind of mad at him for giving me that message, because I was pretty comfortable where I was at, sort of picking and choosing where I wanted to be a Christian or not. So that was a real eye-opening experience and turning point in my life and my faith. That whole year, I had lots of time because I was living on my own, and decided I needed to take a deeper look at my faith. That's when I really started to grow as a Christian. I started looking at this for myself, and that's when it became very important to me.

"**As I made that transition for myself**, that first year of pro, I started learning more and more about God and how to live the right way by reading the Bible and some good devotional books and inspirational Christian sports books. Reading books of other Christian athletes helped me a lot, just hearing these other guys' stories of how they dealt with things. It was very important to me to try to get some of this reading in every day. In those first few years of pro, I found I was hot and cold with my faith. I would be really into it – doing a lot of reading, studying, thinking and praying. Then there'd be a few days or even a couple of weeks where I thought, 'Oh man, I haven't thought about God at all,' and I felt guilty about it. But I've developed a discipline now to always have a devotional book or some Christian literature there at my bedside table, and read a few pages here and there at night or in the morning. I think that has helped me grow in my faith and become aware of temptations, and helped me make good decisions."

Training for Life with Dan Hamhuis:
A favorite verse

Romans 8:28: "And we know that in all things God works for the good of those who love him, who have been called according to his purpose."This verse gives me great peace, knowing that God is in control at all times. Even when things don't go the way I want them to, I trust that God is using those circumstances for good.

Dan also had some great examples who encouraged him in his budding faith along the way. "When I was in Nashville, Greg Johnson and Stu Grimson were there. Greg was our captain and even though Stu was on his way out, he was at training camp and he was around. I saw them around the guys in training camp and how well-respected they were by all of the players. What was interesting about them, was how well they both fit in – everyone wanted to hang out with them, and they are both very strong Christians. They were great examples to me, and showed me how it can work being a Christian in an NHL dressing room. That gave me the courage to say, 'Hey, I can do this.'

"Sometimes I think there's a perception that if you're a Christian in hockey, people will treat you differently or give you a hard time, but actually, some of the guys become quite interested in what you're doing and what's going on at chapel. I think some guys are curious, but they're afraid to come. They think they've done too many bad things. What they don't realize is that it's not about what you've done. By becoming a Christian and accepting Jesus, all your sins are forgiven and you're free. You put your past behind you and move forward in a relationship with Jesus. I think a lot of people worry that they'll have to give up all of the fun things they were doing before and lose all their freedom. But what really happens is that, out of your love for Jesus, you don't really desire those things anymore. Over time, guys really come to respect you for what you believe in and how you live your life, and just being an honest guy. It's never a popular choice when you say you're going to leave the party early and go home. It's always a hard choice, but guys respect it. Being a Christian has helped in difficult times, high pressure times, or even in really good times, because I know that God's in control, and there is such a bigger picture out there to life, other than the hockey world. That helps me get over difficult times quicker and with a positive attitude, and gives me a sense of peace when dealing with those things. In good times too, it helps with not getting too high, and just taking things as they come."

This steadiness has gained Dan attention on the ice too. With a solid faith that forms the foundation of his character, he maintains a strong work ethic, honing his God-given abilities, as demonstrated in his NHL Central Scouting Report: "Dan is a very good, well-balanced skater with good agility and excellent speed...A very skilled, intelligent defenseman who anticipates the play very well and makes good decisions...Has good puckhandling skills and a hard, accurate shot...Is a confident puck carrier and is very capable of leading the offensive rush...Possesses excellent passing skills and is a strong playmaker...Quarterbacks the power-play...Has excellent stamina and logs a tremendous amount of ice-time...A very strong competitor and a hard worker...Plays a very sound positional game and is very poised and efficient in the defensive zone...Is strong in the corners and in front of the net and has shown a mean streak at times...Specializes in the hip-check along the boards and is a very good open-ice hitter." [2]

With skills like these, it's no wonder that Dan Hamhuis has gained the respect of his teammates, as well as recognition from the leagues in which he's played. The list of honors is quite impressive. In the WHL he was awarded rookie of the year, scholastic player of the year two times in a row, most dedicated player, and most valuable player in Prince George. He was also named to the WHL First All-Star Team and presented the Bill Hunter Memorial Trophy and Four Broncos Memorial Trophy as the league's best defenseman and player of the year, respectively. Then in to the Canadian Hockey League, he received the Defenseman of the Year award and was named to the CHL First All-Star Team. In the AHL, he made the Second All-Star Team and played for the Canadian team in the 2005 All-Star Game, and the year prior, played in the NHL Young Stars Game. In international play, Dan helped his team win bronze in 2001, then a silver medal in the 2002 World Junior Championships, and he participated in four straight World Championships, winning gold in 2007 and silver in 2008 and 2009.

Dan has also been a contributing defenseman in the NHL for seven seasons. He was selected twelfth overall by the Nashville Predators in the 2001 Entry Draft and playing with the Predators for six seasons before becoming an unrestricted free agent and signing a six-year contract with the Vancouver Canucks.

And did we mention the Stanley Cup Finals in his first year with Vancouver? "Last year, playing in Vancouver was a dream come true for me. Playing for the team I grew up watching as a kid, and to be able to play so close to home, made for a real fun and exciting year. Vancouver has a great hockey environment to play in and the playoff run last year was a lot of fun to be a part of, excluding the riots of course."

How Does He Do That?
Dan's Special Training Tips

How do you prepare mentally for your games?

Dan: I always pray during the National Anthem. That's a habit I've gotten in over the last three or four years. I really enjoy that. No matter how big of a game it is, or if I'm not really into the game, it always just helps get me centered, just having a quick conversation with God in that moment. The other thing I do every day is to spend about fifteen minutes in prayer – driving to the rink is my prayer time. I just turn off the radio and drive in silence and in prayer for that fifteen minutes. It's such a nice way to start the day, and it's really become a routine, a habit.

But the fun was short-lived for Dan – which brings us to the third memorable time in his career that he would trust the hand of God working through disappointing circumstances. It wasn't a broken leg this time, but a series of injuries throughout his first year with Vancouver right into the Stanley Cup Finals. "There is never a good time to get injured in hockey, and especially being new on the team, it's the last thing I wanted to happen. I had been fortunate to be fairly injury-free throughout my career. To have three pretty serious injuries that year was difficult, but what helped me get through it was trusting that it was God's will. I could have really been down in the dumps, with the bruised foot, and then a concussion. The last injury, I tore my groin and suffered a hernia in game one of the Stanley Cup Finals. That was a really tough one to accept after finally making it to a position to win the Stanley Cup, a goal and dream of mine my whole professional career. But, I just prayed, 'God, I've had bad injuries in my life before that I didn't understand. I don't see why I have to have this now, but I've seen your hand working in my life in other situations just like this, and I'm at ease trusting You and knowing You're in control.' It may be too early to look back and see a clear reason why this had to happen, like when I broke my leg when I was young. Maybe I will never see it. But whatever a day may bring, whether good or bad, it always presents an opportunity to grow stronger as a person and in my faith."

With the 2011-2012 season underway, Dan is happy to be back in the Canucks line-up and hoping to stay healthy from here on out. Looking ahead, he's sure to want another shot at the Stanley Cup, but only time will tell if the ultimate hockey prize is part of the Lord's plan for his life. Looking back at his career, while he certainly has some memorable moments, from all of his honors and awards, to his first game in the NHL, to winning the World Championship with Team Canada. He would readily say that the most rewarding part of his career has been the ability to give back to the communities in which he's played. It's apparent that the spirit of giving runs deep for Dan, as exhibited by how he gives everything he has, both on the ice and off.

"**This career has given me a lot of blessings** and I feel fortunate to be able to give back. My wife and I feel a certain responsibility with what God has given to us to manage it well, whether it's our money, time or influence. We really enjoy trying to make a positive difference in peoples' lives, whether it be within our own families, our local communities, or around the world."

Training for Life with Dan Hamhuis: A favorite verse

Luke 12:48: "...From everyone who has been given much, much will be demanded; and from the one who has been entrusted with much, much more will be asked." This verse helps me keep things in perspective and reminds me that everything I have is from God, and that He expects me to use those things responsibly and wisely.

Dan took a trip to Haiti last summer to see the devastation first hand and help announce the fundraising efforts of the NHLPA for a children's hospital there. The trip has inspired him to use his platform as a Vancouver Canuck to encourage local schools in the Vancouver area with their fundraising for developing countries through World Vision. Dan and his wife Sarah also partnered up with Manny Malhotra and his wife, Joannn, to build a playground for Edmonds Community School, which serves underprivileged children – about 35% of them from refugee families. Dan is aware of the opportunities his position gives him to talk about his faith and encourage young players. "Being a professional athlete, and especially a professional hockey player in a Canadian city, I want to use the influence I have to be an example of Christian living and share my testimony, my story, with young hockey players."

All-in-all, that broken leg at age 14 seems to have worked out pretty well for Dan Hamhuis – having led to a notable hockey career and opportunities to serve and help others. But there was something else that developed from the change of paths that occurred with that broken leg that led Dan to Prince George. Dan met someone whom he may not have otherwise. "I met my wife in Prince George when we were fifteen, and we started dating when we were seventeen. We ended up getting married in Prince George four years later. Sarah and I have been married for seven years now, and she's been through everything with me. Her down-to-earth and caring personality has been such a blessing in my life and the lives of our two young girls, Anna and Morgan. At age three and a half and one and a half they make life interesting, and disconnect me from hockey when I get home from the rink. No matter what kind of day I've had at the rink, they really don't care. When I walk through the door, they're excited. So if I had a bad day, I better put it behind me pretty quick. They want to play dress up in the princess castle and have a tea party with me." Grinning ear to ear, Dan adds, " I've got to refocus on the tea party pretty quickly!

Training for Life with Dan Hamhuis:
A favorite verse

Philippians 4:13 and 2 Timothy 1:7: "I can do everything through him who gives me strength;" and "For God did not give us a spirit of timidity, but a spirit of power, of love and of self-discipline." These two verses are very inspiring to me and give me a strong belief that anything is possible with God.

"As I look back on the path I took to get to the NHL I certainly see God's hand guiding me. The commitments from my parents, the coaches I had, the broken leg, playing in Prince George were all things out of my control. I know God has put me in the position I'm in for a reason. I can see God working, directing my life – sometimes in good ways, sometimes in ways I wouldn't chose – but I try to grow stronger from those experiences and put my trust in Him."

"For I know the plans I have for you," declares the Lord, "plans to prosper you and not to harm you, plans to give you hope and a future." Jeremiah 29:11

Dan Hamhuis

Based on Dan's story and favorite scriptures, how might you answer these questions in reflecting on your own story?

1. Have you ever had to deal with disappointing circumstances that ended up leading to opportunities you might not have had otherwise? What did you learn during these times?
2. What did you dream about doing when you were young? How did you develop the skills and perspectives to allow you to pursue your dream?
3. If you have lived away from home already, what challenges or trials did you experience? How did you handle these? Who helped you through these times?
4. If you have not yet lived away from home, how might Dan's experience help prepare you for this time?
5. Have you ever attended a chapel program? Why or why not? How might Dan's experience and perspectives encourage you?
6. What encouraged you most about Dan's story? What could you relate to the most, and how might some of his experiences and perspectives apply to your life?

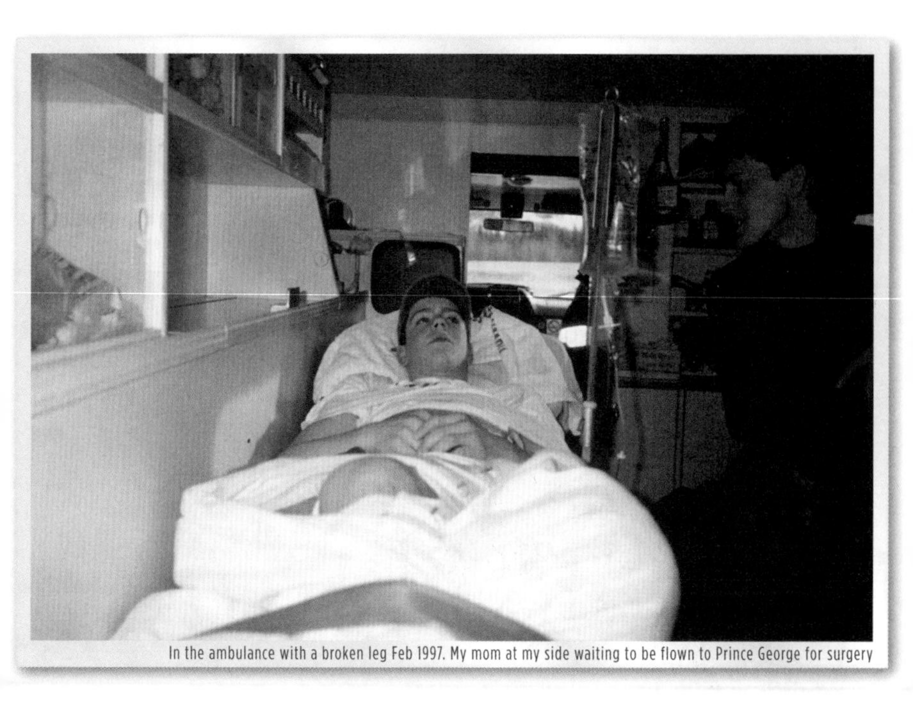

In the ambulance with a broken leg Feb 1997. My mom at my side waiting to be flown to Prince George for surgery

Playing in my driveway with my wheelchair a few months after my broken leg

14 years old reading in my bedroom

Viewpoint on the bluff above Smithers. One of my favourite places to bike

Mike Rupp
71
RANGERS
71
EASTON
EASTON
EASTON

Mike with Christi, Maddie, Mason, and Max

2011 Winter Classic at Heinz Field in Pittsburgh (we're all set)

Disney World in '11

Family vacation in '10

If you script any young hockey player's fantasy *played out in their minds time and time again in family basements, driveways, and frozen backyard ponds, it might go something like this: "He shoots – he scores! Game 7 of the Stanley Cup Finals, folks – he's just won the game and made hockey history!" (Sounds of cheering fans in a sold-out arena...) For Mike Rupp, as a Center for the New Jersey Devils in 2002-03, it went exactly like this, as called by Gary Thorne, 2003 Stanley Cup play-by-play announcer: "Rupp, the young rookie came to the playoffs late for the Devils, but he's played physically big. Friesen, Rupp picks it up, tried to go back for the point, did – White, shot blocked by Niedermayer – Scott Niedermayer – scores! Mike Rupp deflected it!" [3] As it turns out, this was the game winning goal, at 17:38 in the second period of Game 7 against the Anaheim Mighty Ducks, making Mike Rupp the only player in Stanley Cup history to have his first playoff goal and a Stanley Cup winning goal be one in the same. Truly, a young player's fantasy come true, capturing a bit of hockey history to boot.*

Mike Rupp's journey to the Cup, though, began where most hockey dreams begin – in the driveway. "I grew up in Cleveland, Ohio, and I played a number of different sports, but when I was six, my neighbor played hockey in the driveway, and I had never seen it before. That was a time, in the East, when hockey wasn't really played that much, so I never watched it. When I saw this kid in his driveway, I went over to his house and started to play with him. It just kind of went along from there. I didn't really know what I was supposed to do, so my mom thought I should take figure skating lessons to learn how to skate, which was embarrassing.

Fortunately, that was well before camcorders were around! So, I took that for probably a year and a half, and then I started playing. I enjoyed it because it was different. I was one of the only ones in my school who played hockey, and that was kind of neat. So like any kid in any sport, when you think you're pretty good at it, you're going to want to play it more, and that's what happened with hockey."

Every hockey family knows what a commitment it takes for their kids to play. After all, it's not like they can just run outside or down to the neighborhood park, suit up and play. Early mornings, long commutes to ice arenas, travelling for games and tournaments are challenging enough, especially for single-family homes like the one in which Mike grew up. "My mom and dad were divorced when I was in third grade. That was a tough time for my sister and me. It was just one of those times that really changed a lot of our childhood. She made many sacrifices and fought hard for me to play hockey. From the time I was only 12 years old, even though she was working long hours, going to school, and really didn't have any down time, she spent her weekends taking me up to Buffalo for a hockey tournament or staying the weekend with me in Detroit to be able to play in important competitions."

Providing Mike with the opportunities he would need to excel at hockey wasn't the only advantage his mom tried to give him. Even as busy as they were in the Rupp household, Mike's mom did what she could to pass her faith on to her children, taking them to church when the rigorous hockey schedule allowed. "My image of God was that as long as I went to church on Sunday and I did the right things, I'd be OK and doing better than most. My grandmother always had my sister and me watch Cecil B. DeMille's *The Ten Commandments* at her house, and I knew what the Ten Commandments were, so I thought as long as I follow those and do the best I can do, I'll go to heaven. But, mostly I'd have to say, at this point, hockey was my God. Then, when I was 19, all of that changed.

"I was drafted into the NHL when I was 18 – pretty high in the draft. Along with that came some pressures I put on myself. Instead of enjoying it, I allowed it to consume me more. I didn't sign with the NHL team that drafted me, and I didn't know what to do, so in my eyes, I was failing in that moment. I gave up my college, and decided to go and play in the Ontario Hockey League, and by doing that, I really put all of my eggs in one basket. Then things started to go bad with my career. I'd just work at it harder, and try harder, and consume myself with it even more, and I was exhausted. It sounds funny. I was only 19, but I felt like I couldn't work any harder than I was, and I couldn't get it any more into my mind. It was controlling me, and I didn't know what to do. I didn't even know if I was supposed to play hockey. I started questioning God about what His plans were for me. This was a scary time because, ever since I was in the first grade, and the teacher asked us what we wanted to be when we grew up, I always wanted to be a professional hockey player. That was all I ever wanted to be. And here it was, so close, but it just wasn't there for me. I had been so committed to that goal that I really felt like I had nothing else going for me, and I was scared by that.

"**It was also during this time when I met my girlfriend** Christi, who is now my wife. She would ask me questions like whether I had a relationship with God and whether I knew if I was going to heaven, and I didn't even really understand that. So I'd just ask her questions. I was always playing the devil's advocate by asking her what I thought were foolish questions that I thought I knew the answer to. But I needed more evidence of why I needed God. I wanted to understand that better and get closer to God and understand more about this whole Jesus thing. I was just confused and scared.

"**Then we went to a church in Erie, Pennsylvania**, and it was kind of funny because it wasn't the kind of church we'd normally go to – very loud music and all very new to me. But a friend invited us to go, so we went. And the message that day just felt like it was speaking right to me. I just remember the pastor kept saying that Jesus loves you and isn't going to leave you – ever. He kept driving that point home, and it kind of broke me down, and I decided I was ready for this. I was tired of trying to be good to get to go to heaven, and I was tired of trying to be a good hockey player so

I could make it to the NHL. I just wanted to be me, and I wanted that to be enough. So I made a decision right there. The pastor asked everyone to close their eyes and bow their heads, and said if anyone wanted to have a personal relationship with Jesus Christ to say a prayer with him. I stood there and said the prayer of salvation, and asked Jesus into my heart. It was a really emotional time, and after that day, everything changed for me."

Training for Life with Mike Rupp: A favorite verse

1 Peter 5:7: "Cast all your anxiety on him because he cares for you." When I was in my 20's, I used to think I have to please God for Him to take care of me and bless my life – but that's not our God. I can just be myself and humble myself before God, and He loves me the way He loves all of us. He doesn't want anything bad to happen to us. That was a hard thing for me to get over – being fearful of God. I always thought, "Hey, you don't want to make Him mad." You don't want to test God, but I believe this verse is telling us that God loves us and He cares for us, and we can trust Him with our fears.

And change began happening quickly for Mike. "The following year, I went away to go pro, and I went without Christi. That pushed me to make another important decision. I knew fairly early on that I wanted to marry her, and I thought, 'What am I waiting for?' So I proposed to her half way through my first year of pro, and we got married that summer, and she's been with me ever since, traveling around with me in this crazy hockey world. We were married in June of 2001, then my first child, Madeline, was born in November 2002."

Mike's faith continued to grow as it was tested and strengthened by the ups and downs he would experience in the rollercoaster ride that is that "crazy hockey world." "I had been playing two years professionally in the minor leagues, and I just wasn't taking that next step into the NHL. That wasn't my ultimate goal, so I started to slowly take control of hockey again, and it was really frustrating. I got to a point where I had a meeting at the end of the year with my general manager, and I just said, basically that if I wasn't going to make my dream, I would go pursue something else and move on. I was just in a place where I had decided to try one more time and see what happened.

"So going into my third year pro, my team in New Jersey lost one of their players who played in the role and position that I play, so they flew me in in the summer and pretty much told me that this was my chance. I was really encouraged by that, and thought, 'Hey, this must be God opening this door for me.' I remember I went to training camp, and I trained real hard in the summer, then I didn't even get a chance to play in a preseason game. They sent me down – I was the first guy they sent down. I called the GM and said, 'I don't understand. You flew me in, and I thought I was going to have a chance to make this team, and I didn't even get that chance in training camp!' And he told me, 'Just work hard and you'll get your chance some day.' Well, that was not what I wanted to hear. So I just really had a tough time, and I was down in the dumps for a while. I remember one of the only good things at the time was coming home and seeing my daughter and playing with her on the floor. It was one of those perspective things that got me out of a hole. Suddenly, hockey didn't seem that important to me. This was my family and that's all that mattered. I got to a point where I contacted the pro hockey association, which had a program set up for helping players pursue jobs after hockey, so I signed up and got some information about becoming a firefighter. I was going to sign up for a summer fast-track camp that was out in western Canada, and I said to Christi, 'This is it – if it doesn't happen this year, I'm fine with it. I've got everything, with my daughter and my family, and we'll be OK. God will lead us, and we'll be fine.'

How Does He Do That? Mike's Special Training Tips

Do you have any routines you do to intentionally prepare yourself for games?

Mike: I'm not superstitious at all, so I'm always changing up what I do physically to prepare. But I do have one thing I do before every game. During the National Anthem, I just pray. I close my eyes and I say, "Thank you, God, for this moment, and letting me play this game. Thank you for these people, and I pray for you to come into their lives in some way so they just feel your presence. And use me in some way, if needed, and if not, you're more powerful than anything I could do. I just pray that you move in this place, and in these teams – my teammates, the team across the ice – and that you move through this game of hockey. I also pray for a safe, clean, hard-fought game between these teams, and that there are no injuries. I pray for the fans, that no pucks will go flying in the stands. I just pray for all of us, that we just have fun here tonight and you just lead me to play in a way that glorifies you, and you permit me to be a player out here who can be a difference for you." Then the National Anthem's usually finishing up about that time, and I just try to make sure I'm in the right mindset – to take the control off of me and just play well for Him.

"Just for that first half of a season, playing was really a struggle. I just wasn't feeling it. Around the end of November I said, 'Let's put together a push. I'm not going to care about what's going on; I'm not going to care if I have a bad game; I'm not going to care because it's all going to be over at the end of this season anyway.' So I started playing, and I was playing loosely, and I was playing the best hockey of my career. I ended up getting a call on my birthday. So on January 13th, 2003, they called me up to the NHL, and it was pretty awesome. During this time, I was also getting back to God and letting Him hold me up, and I really think that by doing that, I was free to play the game without trying to control it, and it really helped me."

As history will show, 2003 ended up being an even bigger year than Mike could ever have foreseen. "After I got called up on my birthday, I played the last 25 games of the season, and I played really well. I thought that I would probably make the playoff roster, but they left me off. At that point, I'm not playing at all. I'm not even practicing with the team for the playoffs. I was part of what they call in hockey the "black aces," – a group of players who form a practice squad, apart from the rest of the players, and they stay in shape and are ready to step in if like half the team gets the flu or something or is unable to play. There's not really a chance of getting in, but our season was over in the minors, so we didn't have anywhere else to play. So we came in every day and we practiced before the team practiced. They didn't want us around the team or even socializing with them. And it wasn't a real hockey practice. The coach would just put you on the goal line and you'd skate until you were basically sick every day. Then we were staying in hotels, and I thought, 'This is ridiculous – why are we doing this? There would have to be like five injuries for me to play, so why am I skating and beating myself up like this? It's summer time, and there are only a couple more months to enjoy with my family. What am I doing?' But it was so weird. I felt like, 'I just have to do it, I just have to work hard, and I have to fight through this,' even though I didn't really know why. At the time, I just really felt that I was going to learn something from it, and I felt the Lord was telling me to do it and not quit – don't go cutting corners, just do it right.

Training for Life with Mike Rupp: A favorite verse

Psalm 46:10: "Be still, and know that I am God..." This means a lot to me because I have a tendency of not being still and letting Him be God. I always go to this verse when things are so crazy, I don't even know what to do. There's something about just "being still." It's telling me to do nothing, and I feel like I have to squirm and do everything I can to get to a better situation, and I think this verse is saying there really isn't anything I can do. I should just trust in God – He's going to guide me, and He's going to provide. The part that says, "and know I am God" means don't just be still and know that everything's going to be OK, or be still and hope for the best. It's God saying, "Be still. I'm the God of the universe, and I'm in control." That's really comforting to know, and I need to remind myself of that pretty often.

"**And I did. I took it seriously, and I worked hard**. The team got to the finals. Up to this point, I hadn't traveled with the team. Then they said they wanted me and another guy to travel with the team for the finals, just because they were in Anaheim, so if they needed anyone, they wouldn't have to fly someone out. So we were practicing with the team now, and it was encouraging and fun again. We went to the rink with the guys, but I did not have the mindset that I was going to play at all. Before game 4 of the finals, I remember I was thinking, 'Oh, well, I had the popcorn up in the press box last night, maybe I'll have the pretzel with salt tonight,' and the coach came up to me, two hours before the game, and he said, 'Are you ready?' And I said, 'Ready for what?' And he said, 'You're playing – so get ready.'

"It was an amazing experience for me to just get thrown into the game. I just didn't want to make a mistake. I didn't want to be the guy who messed up the goal against and caused a fluke in the game. So I just played in games 4, 5, 6, and 7, and by half way through game 5, I must have been playing pretty well, because the coach moved me up to our top line and the last two games I pretty much played on our top two lines. I was able to enter game 7, and we won that game 3-0. I had a goal and two assists, and it was really something. It was crazy." Wait a minute – Mike had *a* goal? Actually, it was the first goal of the game, which ended up being the game winning goal! He just humbly replies, "The type of player that I am – I don't know – other players who score game-winning goals in the Stanley Cup Finals are like Wayne Gretzky, plenty of them are high-profile players, and that's not me. It just made me stretch."

As fans, we get to see the players skate around the rink, each taking a turn hoisting the Cup high above their heads, jumping all over each other, yelling and cheering – and Mike certainly enjoyed being a part of that. More important to him, though, was finding his family. "It was crazy, like nothing you could imagine. That building was so loud, and I just remember after scoring the goal, my teammates just jumped into my arms, and everyone was so happy when the game was over. The Cup came out, and everyone was passing it around, and it was crazy, because that's what I always played for. But all I remember the whole time was that I just wanted to find Christi and Maddie. They were probably trying to work their way down, and I remember just leaving the ice, and running around the hallways in my equipment, and we were all yelling and high-fiving everyone, and I'm trying to find out where my family's coming down. I just wanted to see them. It was pretty special."

How Does He Do That? Mike's Special Training Tips

What's your approach to your training routine? Do you do anything special that makes you the player you are?

Mike: I think it goes well with work or life in general, that I don't work at things for people to notice me. The work I do when no one's looking is the stuff that makes a difference. With the way I train in hockey, I don't need to train extra hard in front of the coaches, because I know that I train hard when I'm by myself, and that goes a long way. It's the same in life. I also don't need to be on the news when I'm out doing something in the community. That's just something that's important to us, and we're doing it because we know God is watching. That's who I want to live for, and I just need to live the way God intends me to live when no one's looking.

Over the long summer, the Cup craziness had died away a bit, and it was time to begin a new season. "My hockey career was great when I won the Cup. The next year, I started in New Jersey, and had a rough first half of the year, and I got traded half way through the year to Phoenix. As it turned out, that time in Phoenix was great. I was playing a lot, and I was one of the core guys on the team. They told me they had plans for me, signed me to a new contract, and paid me more, just showing they believed in me. I was playing with other believers on the team, and we were plugged in to Chapel, which is something I hadn't had up until this point. We found a great church, met some good people, and even bought a house, which we were told to do. Everything just seemed like it was perfect, like this was where God wanted us to be. At least that's what we thought. And then, all of a sudden, I got traded.

"I ended up not being in Phoenix very long – just a few months of that remaining season, then through training camp, and I was traded to Columbus after the first game with Phoenix. That was really tough. I had to go right away and play with Columbus the next night in a game in Chicago, so I had to leave my wife and kids in Phoenix. We had just bought this house, and we were still unpacking stuff, and we didn't know what the next step was. We really loved it in Phoenix, and we went from complete happiness to complete chaos, frustration and disappointment. It's kind of funny because I grew up in Cleveland, and you'd think it would be like a homecoming. I remember talking with my mom, and she was saying that it would be great for me to come and play with Columbus. At any other time, I would be thrilled to play there, but I really didn't know how to feel at that time. Not only that, but I found out that my time in Columbus was only intended to be brief, and the trade was just of a matter of salary management. They basically told me I wasn't going to play for the rest of the season and they weren't going to re-sign me, so they put me on waivers to give another team the option to pick me up. So now I was just shattered from a hockey standpoint too. It was one of those moments when I was miserable. Christi and I were miserable together. We were miserable hockey-wise, and it was a bad time for us. While I was on waivers, I thought, 'What am I going to do if I never play in the League again? What am I going to do for a living?'

"**Just when I was at this lowest point**, I experienced something that ended up being a big thing for my wife and me. I still remember to this day how we went to a mall playground there in Columbus, and I had my cell phone in my hand, waiting for my agent to call, and it didn't look very good that someone would claim me off waivers. I was sitting on one side of the playground by myself, and Christi was on the other side, and I just put my head in my hands and kind of moaned, 'Oh, what's going on?' Then I happened to look up, and this little girl came running onto the playground. She had Down's Syndrome, and I don't know what else she was dealing with, but she looked like she might have had cancer of some sort because she didn't have any hair or eyebrows. She just came out onto this playground with the biggest, greatest, most loving smile I've ever seen. I remember looking up and seeing her coming straight toward me, and she came over and started playing with my kids, and I thought, 'What am I doing? I do this all the time. I get so wrapped up in this hockey stuff – and this girl is showing the joy of life right now, when she's the one who should be feeling the way I'm feeling.' It was just really one of those perspective things that let me know that I need to let God be God and not try to be God myself. He has a plan for me, and whatever is His plan is His way, and I'm not going to get in His way to change that. In that moment on the playground, that little girl helped me to see that. And I can also say that, looking back on that time in Columbus now, as bad as it seemed, I can't help but see that God's fingerprints were all over the situation that brought me there, even though I couldn't see it at the time."

What Mike couldn't have foreseen was that, while he was in Columbus, he began experiencing increasingly strong episodes of a heart disorder known as Wolff-Parkinson-White Syndrome, first diagnosed at a training camp physical in 1998. "They told me I had this heart disorder. It was something that was not too uncommon, so I should be able to go through my life and my career without having an issue with it. I was having my regular EKGs, and it was showing up in there, but I didn't think anything of it. So I just kept playing. I might notice a few little things here and there – a speeding up of my heart or a little heartbeat irregularity, but I never paid any attention to it. When I was in Columbus, it started getting more frequent. It wasn't anything much. Maybe it would last for an hour, maybe a little less. I had just finished a game at night, and I came home and was just sitting there watching TV. It was weird just sitting there and feeling some chest pain and seeing my heart bouncing around through my shirt. I started sweating, and I thought, 'Oh, here we go – it's on again.' What I'd usually do was try to go to sleep, or do physical activity, which I thought would kind of reset it. That was dumb. I was walking upstairs to go to bed, and I just remember falling on the stairs. Christi came and asked what was wrong, and I said, 'I'm just having one of those things, and I just want to go lay down.' She thought I should go to the hospital, but I was thinking the whole time, 'I can't go to the hospital or I'll never play hockey again. They'll think I'm going to die on the ice or something.' But I told her that if I didn't feel better in the morning, I'd go. The episode went on for twelve hours, and it wasn't getting any better. I didn't get any sleep, and the sheets were covered in sweat. I'd keep passing out if I tried to stand up, so I agreed to go in to the clinic.

"**They hooked me up to the machine**, and my heart rate was pushing almost 300 beats per minute. I didn't know my heart could do that. The doctor told Christi that wasn't good. They didn't have time to get an ambulance there, so she would have to drive me straight to the hospital without stopping, and the doctors there would be waiting for me. When we got there, they checked me for a blood clot, which they told us was starting to form and would have caused a stroke. So they had to shut my body down, stop my heart and use the paddles to reset it and get it going again. They also didn't know that I have atrial fibrillation, and the combination of this with Wolff-Parkinson-White can be deadly, so they told

Christi and me that I was really fortunate to be alive. This was one of those times that just made me think, 'Hockey does not even matter.' We had also just had our second child, Mason, and all of this was a real eye-opener for me and one that has stuck with me the most in realizing that hockey is really not that important in the grand scheme of life.

"**Then they said I had to have a heart procedure**, and the doctor who was renowned for this was in, you guessed it, Cleveland. That's when I started to think that maybe God sent me to Ohio for a reason, to take care of me. How could I not think His hand was in it, when I ended up being only 120 miles away from the very doctor who specialized in the procedure I needed? I'm grateful for that. Even though going to Columbus wasn't my plan, it was the best thing for me. The Lord pulled me out of what I thought was right for me, and clearly put me where He wanted me."

Mike underwent the procedure that has resulted in normal EKGs, and he hasn't had an episode since. Having gone through such a harrowing experience, and being uncertain of a future in professional hockey, some players might think that their hockey careers are surely over, and start counting their blessings for their hard-fought accomplishments. Not Mike Rupp. Instead, he began to focus on how he could continue to develop and what he could uniquely contribute as a valuable member of a team. "I came out of that time thinking, 'Hey, there aren't going to be too many teams that are going to be knocking on my door, after I've had a poor year of playing and then I also had a heart issue.' So I decided that I was going to provide something different. That's one of the huge things in hockey – you don't have to be the best player, you just have to be willing to do the intangibles and do something different. I felt that, with my size, I needed to play more physical. That didn't mean that I was going to go out there and fight all the time. It just meant that I was going to go out and use my size to my advantage and be more demanding in the way I play, and by doing that, draw some attention. This was something that has really helped my career, and playing physical is the foundation of my game now."

Training for Life with Mike Rupp:
A favorite verse

2 Chronicles 15:7: "But as for you, be strong and do not give up, for your work will be rewarded." It's one of the most difficult things in life to continue working hard and staying strong when it seems that God isn't there. Whenever everything seemed to be falling apart in my hockey career and in my story, I didn't give up – I felt like I was being told by God that there's a light that's not too far ahead, and I just needed to keep on working. I didn't always see it in the moment, but I've always felt like that's how God wanted me to handle difficult situations. I often find in my life that the biggest blessings are followed by some trial, or right before a blessing, I went through a trial. That perseverance is something I've definitely learned and I cherish...and I'm still learning.

The physical nature of hockey is often one of the most misunderstood aspects of the game – not to mention the primary cause of ill-informed stereotypes and jokes. Remember the ol' "I went to a fight and a hockey game broke out?" But to the players, having a guy like Mike Rupp on the team is no joke. In fact, the physical players are often the most respected, as they take on the responsibility for protecting teammates and adding an aspect of grittiness to the game that not everyone can bring. "You have to have a certain kind of mindset. Just like when I wanted to be a firefighter, if you have the ability to help other people, then you should do it. I'm not saying in hockey that's always the situation, but if you can, you have to protect your teammates, and I take pride in that. There's a code between players in the league, and it's very real. There's nothing scripted, but there are some unwritten rules that you kind of follow, and you have a respect for guys who fight. I've fought against friends, and I've fought against former teammates. I fought a guy a couple of years ago who came at me twice in one game. But you know, the next year, after a game, I was bringing the kids out of the locker room, and I passed him in the hallway and he shook my hand. We talked like we knew each other. It's the bond you have with these guys. He has respect for me, and I have respect for what he does.

"As far as reconciling his physical game with his faith, Mike acknowledges, "I've taken heat before from people saying, 'How can you call yourself a Christian if you're going to fight?' The fact is that, if fighting was not in the rules of hockey, I wouldn't do it. But I think fighting is important and it has a place in hockey on a bunch of levels – allowing your skilled guys to change the momentum of a game, or letting the opposing team know you're going to be hard to play against. It's tough to play against a team when you know guys will fight you, but it's also in the rules of the game, and those guys have respect for one another. It's an important role. Besides," Mike laughs, "it could be a lot worse. We're skating around with weapons in our hands, and we're shooting a weapon, and we pretty much have knives on our feet! So I think I'd much rather get a punch to the chin than have any of those weapons coming at me."

Mike's strategy paid off, as his physical, hardworking style led to his return to the New Jersey Devils in 2006 under a one-year contract, and then to two more years with the Devils when he resigned in 2007. During this stretch, however, Mike also experienced one of the most dramatic demonstrations of God's grace. One that left a lasting impression, literally, and a reminder of the depth of forgiveness that is available to those who pursue God's heart, even through the trials and failures of life.

Training for Life with Mike Rupp: A favorite verse

Galatians 2:20: "I have been crucified with Christ and I no longer live, but Christ lives in me. The life I live in the body, I live by faith in the Son of God, who loved me and gave himself for me." That's my favorite verse and what I got my tattoos for. As I said before, all of my teammates at the pro level know I'm a Christian – I think that's something people know about me. But I wanted to do something to mark me and remind me – like a reset button – of what Christ did for me and to live my life in integrity for Him. So, in both my wrists, I got a tattoo of a stake going into my wrists, which is obviously for Christ being crucified. Now, when I'm stressing about something or I'm not playing well or things in life are going bad, it's my reset button – it helps me get over some obstacles, because He's bigger.

The incident occurred during game three of the 2008 playoffs between the Devils and the New York Rangers, where Mike was caught on camera trash talking Paul Mara. Everyone slips up and loses control at times, but not everyone has their mistakes instantly broadcast on You Tube and the international news. But once it's "out there," we rarely get to see the impact that "blowing it" has on a person. This mistake definitely took its toll on Mike. "I think you try to be a man of integrity in the things you do, and the worst thing I would ever want to be called is a hypocrite. That's something that's very important to me. We were playing in that playoff game, and the telecast had a microphone over the glass.

There was a scrum, and I was using language I wouldn't normally use. It was just in the heat of the moment.

"Usually, after a game, if I've scored a goal or played a really good game, I'll have a bunch of text messages from my family and friends saying, 'Good job!' or whatever. In this game, I didn't really do anything, but after the game I had like 25 messages and I wondered what was going on. So I started looking, and my mom left one that said, 'I can't believe you said that – I was watching the game with your grandma, and she heard it too.' And I thought, 'Oh my gosh, are you kidding me?' So then I remembered what happened, and my sister left me a message saying that, on the broadcast, the commentating stopped for a second and the volume was perfect, and they could hear just as clear as day what was being said. It was obviously me. The cameras were all over, and I just felt awful. I just felt so bad. I came home, and it was really, *really* bothering me. I went on the computer because someone said it was on You Tube, and I read some of the comments of fans saying, 'This guy's supposed to be a Christian? Give me a break.' I was reading these things, and I thought, 'That's the worst thing I could possibly do is to be a hypocrite,' and it bothered me for a really long time. You know, you talk to some people and they'll tell you not to worry about it, not to sweat it. But that's not me, it's not Mike Rupp. I know I mess up all the time, but by me doing that, it completely demolished anything I was trying to stand for, and that's why I felt so bad. I just felt awful for weeks after.

"**I remember my wife Christi was obviously not very happy** with me either, but she said, 'This is between you and God. You're not perfect, you mess up all the time, you sin, and this is just another one of them. You just have to talk to God and ask Him to forgive you and to strengthen you so you don't do it again.' That was helpful, and it was kind of comforting knowing that He will help get me through. I think, over time, this has shown me that I'm real and these things happen, and God is real, and He never lets go of me. Even when I feel like He should because I'm such an idiot, He doesn't do it. He always brings me back if I go to Him. I've heard pastors in churches spill their guts in their sermons about things they've struggled with, and this makes me know that, even though we live in a fallen world, God's real, and as long as we're pursuing His heart and asking Him to make those changes in us, we're forgiven. Only He can help us through those things."

Mike didn't just chalk up this experience as a lesson learned and move on, however. He wanted to do something tangible that would help him through the day to day challenges and temptations of life. "All of my teammates at the pro level know I'm a Christian. I think that's something people know about me. But I wanted to do something to mark me and remind me of what Christ did for me and to live my life in integrity for Him. So, on both my wrists, I got a tattoo of a stake going into my wrists, which is obviously for Christ being crucified. Now, when I'm stressing about something or I'm not playing well or things in life are going bad, it's my reset button – it helps me get over some obstacles, because He's bigger. My favorite verse is Galatians 2:20, so that's what I got the tattoos for – 'I have been crucified with Christ, and I no longer live, but Christ lives in me.'

"It's easy to say now, and it doesn't feel this way at the time – but when you're going through obstacles and trials, these are the things that are going to help you and strengthen you. Whether it's through hockey, like getting cut from a team or whatever, you feel the pain, but it makes you stronger to demand more from yourself and try to fill in the gaps in your game. That's something that's been big for me – I just try to use those experiences to make me stronger. When there's a trial, it's also an opportunity to see God at work – especially when it's something I know I won't be able to get through by myself. I heard an analogy one time from a former major league baseball player who told me that my relationship with God is like riding a tandem bicycle. There are times when God's in the back of the bike, and I'm in the front seat and pedaling hard and trying to steer where I'm going and trying to take control of the bike. But it's something that has to be done together. When I sit in the back and pedal hard and God is controlling the handlebars and where it goes, the ride is much smoother, and new paths are presented to you."

Training for Life with Mike Rupp: A favorite verse

Colossians 3:23: "Whatever you do, work at it with all your heart, as working for the Lord, not for men." I still trip up and get caught up in hockey, trying to be the best I can be, or trying to be accepted – whether it's by my coaches or teammates. But I seem to muddy up situations by trying to take control of things myself. This is a verse I go to when I need to remind myself that pleasing all of these people is not as important as just living my life to please God.

The new paths presented to Mike came in the form of a two-year contract with the Pittsburgh Penguins, signed on July 1, 2009, and the arrival of his third child, Max, nine days later. During his time with the Pens, Mike recorded his first career hat trick and a career high of eight goals just 28 days into the season. Then, on July 1, 2011, Mike signed his biggest contract yet – three years with the New York Rangers. And he picked up the family and moved once again.

Mike Rupp's journey to the Cup and beyond has taken him a long way from that driveway in Cleveland. The road has been filled with ups and downs, hills and valleys, struggles and joys that would test anyone's resolve. But Mike's life is a picture of perseverance, and he's committed to using his experience and every opportunity the Lord has given him to continue to grow and reach out to others wherever he can make a difference. "I think it's been challenging at times. There are always moments when I go back to trying to grab a hold of everything myself and do everything myself, but it doesn't take too long for everything to fall apart and I'm reminded again of how much I need to let the Lord have control. Taking advantage of the opportunities I have to take a step back and get a perspective on things is so beneficial to me – as a Christian and a hockey player, and as a husband and a father. Sometimes I can so easily get consumed by the world and what I'm doing. That's one of my things. When I do something, I want it to be done a certain way. That's a great asset, but it can also be detrimental to the way I am as a husband or a father, or in my time with the Lord. Marriage was an introduction to me of how I needed to step back, because this wasn't about me anymore, and hockey was not everything. It's important, but it's not everything. I just think God has much more in store for us than simply playing the game.

"**I've been very blessed to be able to play hockey** for a living, and to have the platform that comes with any visibility or recognition that I have. The fact that I'm an NHL nobody and I can start a Twitter account and have 30,000 followers in a couple of months is something that I want to try to use. I remember we did some work with an orphanage in Haiti, and I put a few tweets out about that, and people were writing about how that had touched them or encouraged them. Or when I'm at the rink and people comment, 'Hey, I read that, and it made me want to get involved,' or with a kid at school that wanted to donate money because he had read my tweet, so he got his friends to raise like six dollars – it's those things that make you want to tear up a little bit. I feel like everyone wants to help, but sometimes we get caught up in our own business and we just don't do it. So if I'm an athlete and, for whatever reason, people look up to me because of that, I may as well use that to benefit others and say, 'Hey, check this out, look at the difference we can make to save these peoples' lives,' and 'Hey, let's help these people out. There's devastation here with this hurricane,' or some other natural disaster. Some people just need a ringleader. My ringleader is my wife. She's done that for me. So we can use this platform I've been given to serve others, and I think that makes me feel relevant and like I'm doing the work God put me here for."

"Serve God and serve others" seems to be the theme of Mike Rupp's journey toward the goal – on the ice in his role as a skilled player who gives it all he's got and defends his teammates, as well as off the ice in his role as husband, father and defender of his faith. In hockey and in life, his perspective is the same. "If I can show my heart and try to make a difference to someone, as God wants us to serve each other, and maybe help one person, it's all worthwhile."

"...let us throw off everything that hinders and the sin that so easily entangles, and let us run with perseverance the race marked out for us." Romans 1:12

Mike Rupp

Based on Mike's story and favorite scriptures, how might you answer these questions in reflecting on your own story?

1. Mike said he knew he wanted to be a professional hockey player since the 1st grade – what are the goals and dreams you've had from a young age?

2. What trials and challenges have you faced or are you facing right now in your journey? How might Mike's story encourage you in handling these?

3. What do you do to gain perspective on your life? Has anyone ever challenged you to think about your relationship with God, the way Christi challenged Mike?

4. Have you ever had an experience where you felt like you really messed up? What did you do about it? How did you seek and find forgiveness?

5. What opportunities have been presented to you to make a difference in others' lives?

6. What encouraged you most about Mike's story? What could you relate to the most, and how might some of Mike's experiences and perspectives apply to your life?

1st year playing hockey (age 6) for the Parma Heights Wings (Cleveland, OH)

Mike Rupp, age 6

Me and Mason before Penguins practice

Mason firing pucks during Pens game

Trip to Haiti orphanage with PKF (Pittsburgh Kids Foundation)

Just hanging out getting to spend time with them

Delivering sticks and playing some hockey

Michael Sauer

Curt Sauer (dad), Michael Sauer and Margaret Sauer (mom) getting ready for my First Communion

Michael Sauer in air, Kent Sauer in blue and Kelley Sauer in white, everyone helps set up for the holidays no matter their size

Michael Sauer and Kurt Sauer, doing some sightseeing around the lake

Imagine being the youngest in a family *where your dad was a professional baseball player, your oldest brother was a linebacker in the National Football League and played in a Super Bowl, one of your older brothers played in the East Coast Hockey League and was drafted into the National Hockey League, another older brother played in the NHL Stanley Cup Finals, and both of your sisters were doctors. No pressure, huh? A kid like that could either end up as a "black sheep," or he could be drafted in the 2nd round, 40th overall by the New York Rangers. Guess which one Michael Sauer is?*

With a family like that, Michael was pretty much destined for greatness. But something other than good genes makes him who he is. A strong commitment to faith and family provided the foundation that would form his character and carry him through the trials and challenges of his journey. "Growing up, I had five siblings, and I was the baby, so I was definitely the lowest in the pecking order. Spiritually, we grew up going to church every weekend. We're all really close. We may have had our fights and things growing up, but we all knew each other, loved each other, and found ways to make up. That was something our parents made sure of. Like at dinner, my dad would say, 'You know, friends may come and go, but at the end of the day, you're still family, and you move past your differences and forgive each other, and you never let anything get in between you.' So, he definitely instilled that in us from the beginning. No matter what came up, we knew we had each others' backs and wanted what was best for each other.

"**We were very competitive**. It didn't matter what it was – cards, games – I guess it's at our core that we want to win. We're pretty mild tempered normally, but when we're competing, it's intense. I was the youngest, so I couldn't really get mad. You know, who was I going to get mad at? I was sort of the happy one because there wasn't anybody to beat on. I tried, but it didn't go too far. I knew where I stood and just learned how to handle all of the different personalities and attitudes and temperaments. There were so many with all of the different people in our family. So I learned how to work with them and how to get along. I think that made me well-rounded. I couldn't really get into much conflict, I just had to go with the flow and simply enjoy where I was. They took care of me, and we had fun. I was usually the one thrown in the net. They

would shoot pucks and I would be the goalie, and I didn't get too much sympathy for it. We definitely got tough because we had to be – that's just the way it was. We weren't crazy rough, but we pushed each other around and got bloody knees and bloody noses. It's funny because my mom's just the opposite of that. She's such a sweet lady and so mild tempered, and she really didn't know or care much about sports. She wanted us to be church boys, in choir and theater and playing the piano. That was her dream. We were church boys, and we do sing and we all played piano, but my dad was more into sports, so we went more that way. I'm thankful for my mom, though, that she balanced us out like that.'

For Michael, right behind family, came hockey. "We grew up in a smaller town, about 10,000 people, just outside of St. Cloud, Minnesota. On the pond outside our house, local firemen would come by, and they'd flood it for us in the winter so we could get out there and skate. We'd leave our hose on all night and get up in the morning, and there'd be a clean slate of ice for us to beat up all day. In the cold winters, your hands and toes and your nose would be freezing and your ears numb, but we enjoyed every minute of it, just being outside and playing the game. That's where it began for me. I wasn't actually going to be able to play hockey. All of my brothers and sisters were active in sports, so my parents didn't have enough cars or people to drive me around. Plus, you know hockey's not the cheapest sport by any means. But the neighbor boy played organized hockey, and I was 7 or 8 years old when they were half way through their season, and he said, 'Just come try it. We'll share a stick.' That was pretty late for starting in hockey, but we had some old gear lying around in the garage, and his parents offered to give me a ride to the games, so I said I'd try it. I scored a goal in my very first game. The guys tried to get me to score a goal, so I think they set me up, but I scored, and it was awesome! I played for the remainder of the year, and my parents saw how much I loved it, so like any parent would do, they gave me the means of getting out there and doing it. I'm very blessed for that, since it really took off from there."

Training for Life with Michael Sauer: A favorite verse

John 15:13: "Greater love has no one than this, that he lay down his life for his friends." This is kind of the mentality I have going into every game. Sometimes, it's a little bit of a challenge because you don't know what's going to happen if you go out there and fight. But Christ loves us, and so we love enough to go play and serve the Lord in hockey by protecting our teammates. That's the mindset I try to get into before every game, and that's the beauty of the sport – that you get to. You don't have to, but you get to. Hockey's such an amazing sport for that reason. It allows you to get close and get that bond together on the team and on that level that you can't really get in other sports, because you can't really be selfish when you're fighting for your teammates – especially when you don't win every fight.

Watching his older brothers succeed in professional sports planted the seed that maybe Michael could make a career of it too. But he really didn't get a vision of just how far he could go until high school. "Because my dad played pro baseball, and one of my brothers was in the NFL, and my other brothers were drafted into the NHL, I remember when I was about 13-years-old, people would come up and ask me, 'So, what sport are you going to play?' I would say, 'I don't know'. I really didn't *know*! I guess I kind of thought that if I worked hard, possibilities could open up and good things could happen, but I didn't know which way I wanted to go." Even without a clear direction, Michael kept working, believing that athletics would be in his future somehow. During this time, he received some valuable advice from his brother, Kent, that he has kept with him throughout his career. "I remember when I was 14 or 15, and I worked out with my brother in the weight room for maybe two or three years. I wasn't in that great of shape, and my brother came up to me and said, 'So, you've got maybe two or three years until you're drafted, huh?' And I hadn't really thought of that. Then he said, 'Just think – you're working hard, but somewhere, some place, some kid – either in Russia, Canada, the U.S., your same age – remember maybe he's working harder. You can only control how much effort you put in. You can't control the talents and gifts you've been given, but you can control your effort.' That really pushed me, and it changed my mentality and my perspective on how to train. I think I'm tired now? You know what? I can do more.

"In my freshman year of high school, I thought I'd just see where I was most successful and where my best opportunity was. I was blessed to be pretty successful at all the sports, but in hockey, I think I stood out the most. So I decided I was going to go for a division 1 scholarship. That was my short-term goal for that moment. And then I decided I would go to the Western Hockey League, because the U.S. Hockey League didn't want me in my draft year. Then I had another decision. Do I leave in my junior year to go pursue a dream that's further down the road? Now I've got my sights set on the NHL, but I went with the WHL so I could always go back to school if hockey didn't work out. That was a big thing for my parents – to do well in school and get good grades. They set a high standard, and that pushed me to be able to do a lot, and I knew I could always fall back on school if I needed to. So I got to the WHL, and I think that's when I could start to see where the potential was and where I could go."

How Does He Do That? Michael's Special Training Tips

Do you have any training tips that set you apart from other players?

Michael: I always remember my brother's advice that I mentioned earlier, "If you think you're doing enough, someone out there is doing more." Oh, and, smile! I'll tell you what, when I work, I have to smile – like when I'm bag skating, if you're not smiling, you're miserable. My brother, Kurt, actually taught me that. If you just smile, after a while, the coaches don't know what the heck's going on. Your poor teammates don't know that you're smiling just because you want to, and they think you're doing great when you're really at your worst. But if you smile, you feel better and you carry a good attitude about it. It's a lot easier when you're happy. You may feel like crying, but you can always make yourself smile. One more thing. Growing up, when we were going through hard times or things weren't going well, or we had a bad attitude, my dad would tell us to stand in front of a mirror, and we had to tell ourselves, "I'm a good hockey player, and I'm going to get better." It sounds stupid, and believe me, I thought I sounded pretty stupid, but saying that actually helped me. It made a world of difference.

Michael entered the WHL with the Portland Winterhawks in the 2004-2005 season, and was drafted in the 2005 NHL Entry Draft by the New York Rangers. He played with the Winterhawks, and briefly with the Medicine Hat Tigers, through the end of the 2006-2007 season; then went to the Rangers' American Hockey League affiliate, the Hartford Wolf Pack, for most of the 2007-2008 and 2008-2009 seasons. On March 23, 2009, Michael was called up to the Rangers, and he played his first NHL game on March 24, 2009. This progression makes it sound as if Michael's journey to the NHL was on smooth ice. But dates and places don't always tell the whole story. Little did Michael know that what he was about to experience would put everything he knew and believed to the test, in a big way.

"2007 was my first year pro, and I had a great training camp. The coaches were happy and they seemed so impressed, and I really thought I had a good chance of making the team. I went into training camp expecting to make it, and everything was going great. Then I got sent down in the last cut, and they told me, 'Just keep playing like you are, and you'll be up before you know it,' and I was so excited – it was awesome! Then I went to the AHL, and it's just a different league, and a different experience. You're living on your own, you have money you never had before, and there are a lot more temptations. I was one of the last ones sent down, so I ended up not having a roommate because everybody else had pretty much already grabbed their spots. I started, and the first half of the year was really tough. Of the defensemen, I was one of the worst plus/minuses on the team. I wasn't living up to the expectations of the coaches there, and I wasn't very confident. Everything was sort of turned upside-down, and hockey wasn't even fun. It was terrible. About halfway through the year, I was getting lonely. I was dating at this point, and even though I liked the guys on my team, I just felt distant for some reason. Some of them had their families and other guys liked to go out and party, and I didn't want to do those things. So it was a tough time. I even took a class just to keep busy with my time.

How Does He Do That? Michael's Special Training Tips

How do you maintain your discipline and your physical strength?

Michael: Well, I do not drink excessively, and I rarely have alcohol. I may have a glass of beer or wine, but growing up, my dad taught us that drinking excessively was not going to benefit us or our bodies, especially in hockey. He used to say that alcohol is one thing that can pull you away from all of your dreams, and I knew that drinking would not help me become a professional athlete. It's pretty simple – if you want to have a chance to play in the NHL, or get a scholarship, don't drink. I don't think I was the most talented. I was always a good athlete, but there were kids who were better athletes than I was. There were a lot of things along the way that I didn't follow, and sadly, some of them did, and they never got to play hockey because they didn't put it ahead of those other, less important things. Having made that decision, sometimes it can create some tension with my friends or teammates, if that's what they want to do. They know how I live, so if they want to go out drinking together every night, they know not to call me all the time. That doesn't mean I'm judging them for doing something I don't do. It just means they respect my decision, and we agree that even though we don't do the same things, we can still love each other and respect each other on the ice and off.

"**As the year went on, my games kept getting worse and worse**, and I kept getting lonelier and lonelier. We played a game against Providence, and we lost 6-2. I was a minus 4, and it was just crushing. I felt like I had given up on myself in many ways, and I didn't know what to do. I didn't understand what was happening to me. I know my dad would say, 'think positive, think positive.' He always preached positive thinking, and I believed it, and I knew it was true, but I couldn't apply it. I went home one night, and I called my dad. I was pacing in my room, and I was really depressed. He told me he'd been there, when he was playing pro ball there was a time when, if someone had handed him a plane ticket home and said, 'get out of here', he'd have grabbed that ticket and flown home and never played the game again. That's kind of how I felt, but he told me, again, to think positively, and I just couldn't do it. My hockey was going out the window, I'd lost my college education because I signed an NHL contract, and I was letting lots of different things put pressures on me. I had such an emptiness in my stomach, I actually thought about hurting myself just because I was so empty – like so empty that pain sounded good to me, and it actually made sense to me. And this was not me at all, really not who I am, not who I ever was. But then, instantly, I got this thought, 'No, you will not do that. You're better than that.' And I thought of the mother of my girlfriend Stacey (now my wife) telling me that the Bible is alive, and that if I ever needed the Lord, I should ask the Holy Spirit to guide me.

"**Then I got on my bed, and I was crying, and I said, 'You know what, Lord**, if there was ever a moment in my life when I needed you, it's now. I'm doing all of this – I'm not having sex, I'm not living with my girlfriend, I'm not abusing alcohol, I'm being as responsible as I can, and I can't get any lower. I need you now.' Then I opened up the Bible, and I happened to open it up to Hebrews 13:5, and it said, '...never will I leave you; never will I forsake you.' It just pierced me, and I felt, wow, just wow. Then I was weeping like crazy, and I couldn't believe God just said that to me – 'I'll never leave you...' At that moment, there was such a presence in that room, and I kept thinking, 'keep reading, keep reading,' so I began to read Hebrews 13:6, and it says, 'The Lord is my helper; I will not be afraid. What can man do to me?' Up to that point, I had been so into my hockey, and I was just trying to please people, like my coaches and my teammates. I was trying to do all this stuff, and it was almost my demise. I was trying to please everybody, but I was killing myself when I couldn't. And I was giving them so much power over me, because if they were disappointed in me, it would crush me. From that moment on, it occurred to me that the Lord is in control, He is in control of my career, and I'm to give it to Him, let Him lead it, and that's all that matters.

Training for Life with Michael Sauer: A favorite verse

Hebrews 13:5-6: " ...Never will I leave you; never will I forsake you. So we say with confidence, 'The Lord is my helper; I will not be afraid. What can man do to me?" Like I said earlier, this is one where I learned that the Lord is in control, and I stopped giving other people power over me by trying to please them and being crushed if I disappointed them. He is in control, and I'm going to give everything to Him.

"**That was such a huge transition in everything for me**, even in my hockey. I went from being the worst plus/minus to almost being out of the minus. My game had changed, my perspective had changed, my life had changed It was such a big day for me because I had gone from a point where I was ready to throw it all away, to all of a sudden receiving something from the Lord like that and knowing that this is where He had called me and how He wanted me to handle it."

Training for Life with Michael Sauer: A favorite verse

Life perspective:

Philippians 4:8: "Finally, brothers, whatever is true, whatever is noble, whatever is right, whatever is pure, whatever is lovely, whatever is admirable – if anything is excellent or praiseworthy – think about such things." My dad was a big believer in positive thinking. I think that's a big reason why we were successful to some degree. He had enough wisdom to be sure we always thought positively. We could never come off the ice and say we had a bad game and he would say, "You can just tell me you could play better." That was the first time I realized that positive thinking is the mind of Christ, so that's what He wants us to think about.

No sooner had Michael overcome one obstacle, however, when he ran head-on into another. "So now hockey's going great, everything's changed, my perspective has changed to where I'm not living to please others, but to please the Lord, things are turned back around, and in the second playoff game of that season I get hit and blow out my knee. I'm thinking, 'Oh my gosh. Are you kidding me?' My knee's totally out – ACL, MCL, a little bit of the LCL. It was just totally shot. I'd already had two surgeries in the past, and I had a concussion that year. What do I do? I remember I thought I was done. I didn't have the greatest year, and now my knee was out. There were a lot of prayers at that time. I know my mom and dad were praying for me. I just didn't know what to do or where to go. I talked to my sister, Christine, and she'd had four knee surgeries in high school, as a soccer player. She was an outstanding soccer player. She was a star. She quit after her junior year, and when I asked her how she knew it was time to quit, she said she just heard like a little voice telling her, 'you're done,' and she just had a peace about being done. And as much as it hurt, she knew it was right. I remember leaving that conversation and thinking that I had never heard that little voice saying, 'that's it, you're finished, there's no more'. So I decided to give it my all again. I followed my mom's advice to prepare for training camp as if I were getting ready to go, even though I didn't think I would be ready to go. I was going to do everything I could to be ready to play. I did the rehab, and it went really smoothly, and I went to camp.

"**Training camp that year was the longest one ever for me**. I was up early every day, and I didn't have a day off for about two months, but I just persevered with a joyful heart, and kept going, and kept trusting that the Lord has a great plan for me, like He says. Hockey went really well, and I started to play really well. Everything started clicking on the ice and I was getting some points, getting some pluses. We were about three months into the season, and other guys were playing as well or better than me, and all of the sudden, I got the call up to the NHL.

"That was a big experience. I get my first call-up, and everything's going great, and then I get sent back down. I didn't play well the first couple of shifts of the game, and I sat on the bench for about 57 minutes, so it was not a good "send-down to the minors" for sure. It was actually really troubling. I was in the town car back to my car, and I was talking to my dad on the phone, telling him, 'I know God has a good plan for me, but I don't know what He's thinking. This doesn't make any sense, but I know He's doing something, and I know I'm going to hang with Him through this, and I'm going to praise Him no matter what this is. He's still good, He's still so awesome, He still loves me, and He still has something good for me.' The woman driving the car overheard me, so she started encouraging me and pumping me up and telling me the Lord has great things in store for me. She gave me Psalm 88, where the psalmist was also in a tough spot and crying out, and it really resonated with me. So, I went back down to the minors, and I played. I also didn't get hurt that year, so everything went pretty well.

Training for Life with Michael Sauer: A favorite verse

Romans 8:1: "Therefore, there is now no condemnation for those who are in Christ Jesus..." With no condemnation, I don't always have to feel bad or guilty when I make a mistake. When I sin or I do something wrong, in Him I don't have those thoughts of, "you're terrible, you're useless, you're a failure, you can't do it," because the Lord is pointing out to me that He knows I'm capable of so much better, and He has something better for me because of what He's done for me.

"Then summer came, and it was a new season, and I had high expectations. I was one of the only D-men called up that year, so I was hoping to make the team again. I went into camp, and it didn't happen. I got sent down right away – *right away* – I wasn't even one of the last ones cut. It was my worst cut ever, and I thought I did well. I didn't understand what was going on, but I just hung with God through it. I went down and played, and I played pretty well – not outstanding, but I still felt like I was capable of playing at the next level. Then I got hurt. I went to hit somebody, and hurt my shoulder. I went to the MRI guy, and he said it's not good at all, that I need surgery, and I'm done.

"**So now I had this injury burden again**. But one thing I learned in all of those past injuries was that, when things go so low, when they seem hopeless, like I don't really have a chance, that if I just praise the Lord in that moment, it takes a burden off my heart. Even though my circumstances didn't change, my perspective did, and I could still praise Him, even though things weren't going perfectly. I told my brother, Kurt, 'This is ridiculous – I'm hurt again? Either I'm going to get healed because the Lord is going to do something miraculous, or it's going to be the worst thing they've ever seen and I'm done.' And it was cool because when they did the surgery, it wasn't nearly as extensive as they thought, and that kind of surprised them. That was really exciting for me, because I was thinking it was the worst injury ever, and I wasn't even sure if my arm was really going to work that well. And now, all of a sudden, they were saying it's going to be a breeze to rehab, and praise God! As I was hanging in there and reading the Word, I had a couple of "go to" scriptures. One was 1 Thessalonians 5:18 that talks about being thankful in all circumstances, thanking God for everything that He's done, and praising Him. Then also, in Philippians, it talks about what we should be thinking about – 'whatever is true, noble, right, pure, lovely, admirable...' Those were big scriptures that I held on to, as well as John 16:33, 'In this world, you will have trouble. But take heart! I have overcome the world,' and James 1, 'Consider it pure joy whenever you face trials of many kinds...' It's amazing how you can apply this to whatever situation you're faced with. No matter how dire it looks, the Word of God can put you in a perspective where you're still joyful and excited about what He's going to show you through these times, and about what's coming. I took the mentality of 'I don't know what you're going to do with this, but I am so excited for it,' and I held on to that and turned to rejoicing rather than sorrow and pain. Yeah, I definitely had my grieving times, but I made sure I was rejoicing for how good He is and where He was taking me. No matter if it was in hockey, or in school, or wherever, I just knew it was going to be awesome.

Training for Life with Michael Sauer: A favorite verse

Galatians 5:22-23: "But the fruit of the Spirit is love, joy, peace, patience, kindness, goodness, faithfulness, gentleness and self-control. Against such things there is no law." This was a revelation to me because when Jesus prays, "Thy Kingdom come, Thy will be done on earth as it is in heaven," He reveals the Kingdom here on earth. And through these fruits there's an inheritance in the Kingdom here on earth that's for me. When we're not bearing these fruits – like with jealousy and anger and hatred – we need to be aware of it, and ask God to help us overcome these temptations. Jealousy was something I dealt with in my walk. So if I was jealous, like if a teammate got called up, the only way I could fight the jealousy was to bless the person. I could try not to be jealous, but that didn't work. I had to act in a way that would counter the jealousy, so I would encourage them and begin to lift them up. And in turn, when I did that, I blessed myself! All of a sudden, I got lifted up, and I was doing better. So I have an inheritance here if I bear good fruit, so I'm going to align myself with that.

"**And then I had my shoulder surgery**, and, again, I didn't hear that voice telling me, 'you're done'. In fact, I felt now more than ever, the Lord was really there, calling me to stay. I didn't feel like it was the end. I felt like there was still more that He had for me, even though my circumstances looked like there was not much left. I just hung in His Word, and I continued to learn about Him and experience Him, and it got to a point where hockey wasn't nearly as big of a god as I had probably made it at one time. It was obviously a big dream of mine, and it was a goal, but it wasn't everything.

Training for Life with Michael Sauer: A favorite verse

Psalm 91:1-16: "He who dwells in the shelter of the Most High will rest in the shadow of the Almighty. I will say of the Lord, "He is my refuge and my fortress, my God, in whom I trust..."Because he loves me," says the Lord, "I will rescue him; I will protect him, for he acknowledges my name. He will call upon me, and I will answer him, I will be with him in trouble, I will deliver him and honor him. With long life will I satisfy him and show him my salvation."

Game Day: These are my game day scriptures – they really put me in the mode of trusting in the power of God and that He's there with me. Psalm 91 is my game day one. I read that every day, before every game, and every time I go on the ice. Then before each game, I have a little thing that I do, where I grab my stick, and I use it to pray out all of my anxieties and fears, and I pray, "Lord, you gave me a stick to use, so I'm going to use this for Your Glory, and I give You all of my fears, all my anxieties, all my worries, and I'm going to go out there and I'm going to serve You today." Praying with my stick is a helpful reminder for me to know that He's with me, He's got me, this is what He wants me to be doing, and this is how I can serve Him. That's what it comes down to – that I can serve Him and bless Him by how I play.

Nothing's worth anything without Him, I guess that's the core of it. Whether it's money, fame, hockey, it doesn't matter. If He's not at the center of it, it's not fun. You can drift away, or maybe you're not even walking with Him, but it's so much more exciting and powerful when you're experiencing Him. He's revealed that to me, and He's still teaching me about that in my journey."

Michael's hockey journey has indeed revealed that more is in store for him, having healed from shoulder surgery, and starting the 2010-2011 season with the Rangers, scoring his first NHL goal on December 9, playing in 76 games and ending the season with a +20 rating. This performance resulted in a two year contract with the Rangers, which he signed on July 8, 2011.

At the age of 24 and with a new season stretched out before him, Michael knows from experience that his journey toward the ultimate goal will not always be a smooth one. Persevering through disappointments and injuries helped him to grow and stretch in his hockey, as he learned how to give his career to the Lord and discovered new revelations about His will and His care. But it was actually a battle that began when Michael was quite young that taught him about perseverance for the sake of a cause higher than himself, and that the power of believing God's promises could get him through anything life might throw at him.

"**In my journey, this is the battle** – this was the fight, and it was an all-out war. There were so many lessons, and different lies I believed about what guys talked about and what guys did that put pressure on me, and so many temptations that led me into something because I was so insecure. Here it is – when I was twelve years old, I was tempted to look at pornography. It was all around me, and I had a real struggle because I also respected women. I didn't understand the temptation side of it, and I didn't understand what you go through as you're becoming a man. I know there are many other people who experience this too. If I can help one person, I am willing to share this.

I believed so many lies, and I had so many questions that seemed like silly questions that I didn't have the courage to ask somebody. You know, as a young boy it is embarrassing. And so it started creeping in. It went from watching a T.V. program that wasn't appropriate to watching a movie, to getting exposed to pornography on the internet and downloading things. At 16 or 17 years old, I remember watching and thinking, 'this does not feel like it used to, and I need more.' Every time I did it I felt empty. I lied to myself for a few years and never felt resolved, until I finally got to a point where I said to myself, 'no more'. Once I realized I was actually hurting myself, and what I thought was helping me was really taking away from my future marriage, I quit. (I had already made the decision not to have sex before marriage). But I remember how I fought with it. I battled to stay away from it. The first step was to delete a program off my computer, and it went on from there. I had to just really trust that the Lord would help me. That was tough to do, but I did the best I could. But the more I experienced Him and kept real with Him, and the more I learned how much He loved me, the more convicted I became.

Training for Life with Michael Sauer:
A favorite verse

Proverbs 3:1-35: "My son, do not forget my teaching, but keep my commands in your heart, for they will prolong your life many years and bring you prosperity... The wise inherit honor, but fools he holds up to shame."

"Then about six months later, I met my wife Stacey. We started dating, and this raised new questions for me about how we should be dating, so I could show her how much I loved and respected her. I was driving home after the hockey season, my second year pro, and listening to worship music, and the Lord was just weighing on my heart. It seems that when you're at a certain moment in your life or in a certain battle or struggle, the Lord reveals things to you that are so powerful and so specific to that one thing. He revealed 1 Thessalonians 4:3 where it says, "...you should avoid sexual immorality...learn to control your own body...not in passionate lust..." So in that moment, I was totally convicted, and, again, I just wanted to put that Scripture into my actions and have control over myself and love my wife for who she is, and be her friend above all else. Obviously, she was on board with that, and the Lord helped us in so many ways get to our goal. Probably the biggest lesson of my life was to trust Him to take care of us, and to step out in faith that He would do what He promised.

Training for Life with Michael Sauer:
A favorite verse

Psalm 121:1-8: "I lift up my eyes to the hills – where does my help come from? My help comes from the Lord, the Maker of heaven and earth...The Lord will keep you from all harm – he will watch over your life; the Lord will watch over your coming and going both now and forevermore."

"**I learned that whenever it would get tough, reading scripture would give me peace**, and it was amazing what He showed me. I also obviously had to be careful about what I'd let my eyes see – I was really seeing the influence of what I was putting into my head. But I kept working on it and praying and reading scripture.

"That was my experience with a really hard struggle in my life for a long time. But I got to really love my wife. We worked together as a team, and it brought us closer together. I could be very open with her because I had to be, and she was very respectful of what I was going through and she helped me. We went through our courtship that way, then our engagement. And we could see the Lord working through us too, as He brought our relationship even closer and made it the way it was supposed to be.

Training for Life with Michael Sauer: A favorite verse

James 1:2-4: "Consider it pure joy, my brothers, whenever you face trials of many kinds, because you know the testing of your faith develops perseverance. Perseverance must finish its work so that you may be mature and complete, not lacking anything."

These are the scriptures I went to whenever I got injured – these are the ones that totally kept me in a rejoicing spirit, even though the circumstances were not perfect. If I didn't know what tomorrow held, I was still rejoicing because He is real, He did it all for us, and His Holy Spirit was working in me:

"**The Lord taught me so much**, from when I was a 17 year old boy and God wasn't even real to me, to experiencing the Lord in my life in a way that I really believed and couldn't argue against. I could try to lie about it or deceive myself, but I couldn't because I knew I was uneasy when I was doing something I shouldn't be doing. It was awesome just to get to the point where I know that whatever's happening, if something isn't going well, I've got to go to God with it and go to prayer and figure it out. And I'm still learning every day. I think that's the beauty of it. With each step, there's something new and more revelation in the guidance He gives you and even the time it takes for something to set in; otherwise, you just look past it and forget whatever happened. But nonetheless, the journey's amazing and the blessings are definitely there."

Training for Life with Michael Sauer: A favorite verse

1 Thessalonians 5:16-18: "Be joyful always, pray continuously, give thanks in all circumstances, for this is God's will for you in Christ Jesus."

What the future holds for Michael Sauer, or anyone for that matter, no one can say for sure. But what Michael does know is the power of perseverance and resolve, as he's experienced in his life, his faith, and his hockey. And he's committed to putting his heart and soul into every game, and continuing to serve his teammates, and others, as best he can. He's also putting his experience and the lessons of his journey to work, as he helps young hockey players build their skills and their faith through Hockey Ministries International summer hockey camps. "The hockey camp is awesome. It's my favorite by far. When I grew up, we never did camps. My dad just basically said, 'If you want hockey, go play with your brothers.' But this camp can be a life-changer. It's so powerful. When you go into the huddle groups and you hear these kids open up their hearts and share their struggles with their buddies, it's amazing that they're able to be so real with us and each other. It took me a long time to feel like I could share that kind of stuff with anybody. The people there are so inviting and so comforting. They truly want what's best for these kids, and they want to help them. It's so Christ-centered, like He's everything at that camp, and that's what I love too. I never grew up knowing a lot of strong Christians in hockey. I knew some, but we didn't talk about it a lot. To see these kids having open conversations, being themselves and being accepted and growing as people as well as in their hockey, is awesome.

Training for Life with Michael Sauer:
A favorite verse

John 16:33: "I have told you these things, so that in me you may have peace. In this world you will have trouble. But take heart! I have overcome the world."

"Everyone comes from all different facets of life, different home styles, different schools. This year, one young boy came from a very tough home, and when he shared that, I was just drawn by his story and how he came to Christ and finally has hope. I know what it's like to not have hope and to feel so empty, and you could just see him 'get it.' I know he may have a lot coming against him, but when he really stepped forth and accepted the Lord and I got to pray with him and talk with him and work with him, it was really powerful. I came from a pretty solid family background, and we always had enough, we always had what we needed and a lot of what we wanted, and we were able to go after things. Not all kids are that fortunate, but there's still a great calling on their lives, and watching them come to the Lord is so powerful and amazing. Obviously, going on the ice and playing capture the flag and all of that is fun too, but hearing the kids' testimonies and how everyone is at their own stage is fun too. I just like spending time with the kids, and I want them to see that I'm here like everybody else. I've been blessed with this gift, and the Lord has helped me to get where I am, and He will help them too – with whatever He has planned for them."

Coming back to that solid family foundation, Michael is thankful that no matter what he goes through or where his career takes him, his family will always be there for him, spurring him on and keeping him humble. "It all comes back to my family. Family is such a great support system. There's something about my family. We've been blessed to be successful in athletics. Sometimes, the world will try to put you on a pedestal, but to them, you're just any normal person, and it's great to come home to that. They'll give you a hard time, and they don't treat you any different if you make a million dollars, or if you're jobless. They're just always there to support each other. I remember when I was sixteen years old, my uncle grabbed hold of me and said, 'Don't ever forget where you came from. And if you ever come back with too big of a head, we'll pop it.' They wanted us to be confident in what we did, but not to get ahead of ourselves. If I did, they'd be the first ones to set me straight. They only did it because they loved me, and it's definitely a way of caring. And it's really cool to be able to come back and just be myself – the fun guy who likes to hang out, play games, play with my nieces and nephews and just be an uncle. That's what I enjoy. And talking about the things I love most – hunting, fishing, hockey and the Lord!"

"Run in such a way as to get the prize. Everyone who competes in the games goes into strict training. They do it to get a crown that will not last; but we do it to get a crown that will last forever." 1 Corinthians 9:24-25

Michael Sauer

Based on Michael's story and favorite scriptures, how might you answer these questions in reflecting on your own story?

1. What role does your family play in your journey? How do they encourage you? What lessons have you learned from your parents?

2. Michael had several experiences going back and forth between leagues before he made it to the NHL. What experiences have you had in your journey, and how might Michael's perspectives encourage you?

3. Have you ever had to deal with injuries? How did you handle them? What insights did you gain, or what lessons did you learn through your injuries?

4. What types of struggles have you had in your journey? How might Michael's story encourage you in handling these?

5. Where do you go for help in handling life's difficulties? Have you ever considered going to God in prayer, or reading His Word for help?

6. What encouraged you most about Michael's story? What could you relate to the most, and how might some of his experiences and perspectives apply to your life?

Christine Sauer and Michael Sauer, showing off our cool rides and how we match them!

Michael Sauer, a successful day of hunting in the bitter cold

David Hines, Charlie Doth, Michael Sauer and Charlie Binsfeld hanging out after school playing some hockey in our front yard

Curt Sauer and Margaret Sauer, all dressed up for a wedding

Michael, Christine, Kurt, Kent, Kelley and Craig. Everyone is home at the same time, so why not take a picture!

NHL Ironman

Doug Jarvis

CCM
BAUER
EASTON
SHER-WOOD
22

Webster's dictionary defines *perseverance* as "continued effort to do or achieve something despite difficulties, failure, or opposition." *While perseverance is necessary for anyone to achieve his or her goals, it certainly describes a 5'9", 170-pound center iceman who, despite being thought by many to be too small to play professional hockey, broke into the NHL with the Montreal Canadiens as the 1975-76 season opened. He was in his team's lineup for the next 964 consecutive games. This amazing "NHL Ironman" record may never be surpassed. The highly skilled and reliable center iceman became part of a legendary checking line and penalty-killing unit. In his first four seasons in the NHL, he played a significant role in helping his Montreal Canadiens win four consecutive Stanley Cup Championships.*

While solid in all aspects of the game, he became one of the best defensive players in the NHL. In 1984 he received the Frank J. Selke Trophy for the forward who best excels in the defensive aspects of the game. He was also an honored recipient of the Bill Masterton Memorial Trophy in 1987, which is given to the player who best exemplifies sportsmanship, dedication to hockey, and perseverance. Given this story line, maybe Webster should add a picture of Doug Jarvis next to that definition.

The strong skater and adept stickhandler began his hockey career in the Ontario Hockey League with the Peterborough Petes. He represented Canada in the 1974 World Junior Ice Hockey Championships where his performance gained him recognition amongst NHL scouts. His selection to the Ontario Major Junior Hockey League Second All-Star Team in 1975 led to his being picked 24th overall by the Toronto Maple Leafs, his favorite boyhood team.

DOUG JARVIS

Boston Bruins

Coach | Shoots: Right
SIZE: 5'9" | WEIGHT: 170 LBS

BORN: MARCH 24, 1955
Brantford, Ontario, Canada

First NHL Season: 1975-76

Last NHL Season: 1987-88

NHL Teams Played For:
Montreal Canadiens
Washington Capitols
Hartford Whalers

NHL Totals (Regular Season and Playoffs):

Games:	1069	Assists:	291
Goals:	153		

AHL Head Coach:
Hamilton Bulldogs: 2003-2005

NHL Teams, Assistant Coach:
Minnesota North Stars/Dallas Stars: 1988-2002
Montreal Canadiens: 2005-2009
Boston Bruins: 2010-present

Honors/Awards:

Frank Selke Trophy (1984)

Bill Masterton Memorial Trophy (1987)

Stanley Cup champion (1976, 1977, 1978, 1979 – as player)

Stanley Cup champion (1999, 2011 – as assistant coach)

NHL Ironman record: 964 consecutive games played

He never got to play in a Leafs jersey, however, since he was traded almost immediately to the Montreal Canadiens, where he played for seven years and established himself in his defensive role, as a premier checking center and penalty killer. In 1982, Doug was traded to the Washington Capitals, where he continued to bolster the defense and help take the Caps to the Stanley Cup playoffs all four seasons for which he played with them.

Then, midway through the 1985-86 season, Doug was inexplicably traded to the Hartford Whalers, which is where he set that 964 consecutive game Ironman record, considerably breaking the previous record of 914.

Shortly after retiring as a player, Doug became an assistant coach with the Minnesota North Stars, helping them make the Stanley Cup Finals in 1991; and he moved with the team to Dallas where they became the Dallas Stars and won their first franchise Stanley Cup in 1999. He stayed with the North Stars/Stars team for fourteen seasons, which is the longest tenure of any assistant coach with the same team. He left Dallas for the head coaching position with the Hamilton Bulldogs, for the American Hockey League affiliate of his former team, the Montreal Canadiens'. They ended up with a 2 year record of 79-54-10-17 under Coach Jarvis' leadership. In 2005, Doug was promoted to an assistant coach with the Canadiens, who made the Stanley Cup playoffs three of the four seasons he was with them. Then on August 4, 2010, Doug was named assistant coach of the Boston Bruins. You may know them as the 2010-11 Stanley Cup Champions.

Yes, perseverance is a quality Doug Jarvis knows a little something about – so when he writes on the subject, we can be assured that we are about to get wisdom that was born out of not only surviving, but growing and thriving in times of "difficulties, failure, or opposition." And we can learn what perseverance has to do with character, maturity, and a life well-lived.

In his own words, "the Ironman" himself shares his views on perseverance:

> *"When someone sets out to achieve a particular goal, he will undoubtedly devise a plan and set himself to that end. It is almost certain that unforeseen detours or unexpected obstacles will present themselves along the way. Consciously or subconsciously, the question, "Should I quit or change my course?" will begin to play on the mind.*

"I really do not know why some people change their minds and quit in the face of adversity while others push ahead. No doubt, one's genetic make-up would offer some clue – but beyond heredity, I suspect that environment would play a key role. It is common knowledge that the atmosphere of the home and the influence of role models, such as parents, will have a profound effect on the development of an individual. Long before the NHL, I was drafted by 'Team Jarvis' in 1955, and the team was made up of my Mom, Dad and my older brother, Howard. They became my first coaches in the all-important game of life. My parents were great role models, and their lifestyle, choices and sense of commitment have had a dramatic effect on my life. My parent's faith in God was evidenced in many areas of their lives and they faithfully attended and were active participants in our church. They were steadfastly devoted to one another and enjoyed sixty-five years of marriage before my father's passing in 2008. Through their words and deeds, I learned valuable lessons about commitment and the importance of perseverance.

"I can vividly remember that as a twelve year old, I was excited about the prospect of having a paper route and earning my own money. My parents advice to me was, "If you decide to take it, then you have to keep it for two years." I didn't foresee any problem with that, and all went well until the beginning of the second year. The afternoon paper delivery interfered with my high school sports schedule, and I clearly recall the ongoing challenge of figuring out how to do both. I will also never forget the sense of relief at having completed the two year commitment and giving up the route. I don't know if my folks ever felt tempted to give in to my appeals and let me off of the proverbial hook, but I am grateful that they didn't. I am thankful that they did not consider it their responsibility to provide a way out or offer excuses for anything less than my best effort. As a young boy, I not only got to experience the sense of accomplishment that comes from seeing a task through to completion, but I also learned that there was a cost to commitment and it was wise to consider this before jumping in. I developed a respect for the authority of my parents and experienced the blessing found in obedience.

"The paper route experience was just one example of the many opportunities that my parents used to teach me valuable, lasting lessons. From their example, and later as a result of my own decision to become a Christian, I understood that my life was not my own, but rather it belonged to God and He had a plan for me. Worthwhile endeavors rarely yield instantly gratifying results, and most challenges require a marathon mentality rather than a sprint mindset.

"**In my own personal life as a husband and father**, I have endeavored to apply these truths. I have to continually remind myself of my goal to keep my wife and family a high priority, in spite of the ever-present challenges of everyday life and work in professional sports. Busy schedules, seven-day work weeks, road trips, fatigue, injuries, slumps, trades and firings are just a few of the pressures and distractions that can undermine my purpose to be all I want to be for my family.

"Throughout my years playing in the NHL, my objective each season was to dedicate myself to being the best that I could be, in order to help my team win the Stanley Cup. As a player, I strove to be a good, honest teammate, focusing on being in good shape physically, mentally and spiritually so that I could give my best effort every game and know that I had done so. There were personal challenges along the way that threatened to defeat me. I knew to expect such obstacles, and I had learned to refocus and to look to God for guidance and the strength to keep going.

"**Like many young boys, I dreamed of playing in the NHL**, but I never imagined playing thirteen seasons and winning four Stanley Cups while doing so. I honestly cannot account for how or why I managed to reach the 964-consecutive-game-streak, except to say that I was blessed to avoid a serious injury, and perhaps those childhood lessons on perseverance paid off. Following my playing career, I have been privileged to coach for the past twenty-two seasons with a number of NHL clubs.

"Thirty-six years ago, I embarked on a professional hockey career that has taken my family and me to numerous cities and offered us many amazing and challenging experiences. As I reflect on my life, I wonder what it would have been like without the game of hockey. About forty-six years ago, I made a decision to accept Christ into my life and to become a Christian. I have been through some amazing and challenging times in my walk with the Lord. As I reflect on my life, I would not want to imagine what it would be without my faith in God.

"Therefore, since we are surrounded by such a great cloud of witnesses, let us throw off everything that hinders and the sin that so easily entangles, and let us run with perseverance the race marked out for us. Let us fix our eyes on Jesus, the author and perfecter of our faith..." (Hebrews 12:1-2)

"**I find these words from the book of Hebrews both challenging and encouraging.** First of all, as I consider those clouds of witnesses, I think about the responsibility that their presence imposes. I remember how daunting and motivating it was to play in front of a sell-out crowd. Just as a player, I had to get into shape and maintain my conditioning, as a Christian, I must continually get rid of those things that impede my spiritual growth. I have learned that I can expect obstacles and challenges that will threaten to defeat me spiritually, and so I must run my spiritual race with perseverance. In hockey and in life, I have learned that the best way to stay the course is to stay focused and keep my eyes on the goal. That goal is Jesus Christ working in and though me to live and to act according to His will.

"The Stanley Cup is a storied and prestigious trophy, and winning it requires that your team persevere and prevail after close to a hundred games, over three hundred periods and thousands of shifts in just one season. It demands countless hours of preparation, dedication and work by individuals you never see on television, and it takes everyone in the organization pulling together to win the race to the Stanley Cup. It is no wonder that winning it leaves you with a sense of excitement and satisfaction. I have had the privilege to hoist the Stanley Cup six times now, and it is an exhilarating experience that admittedly soon becomes a distant memory.

"But there is another race that must be run with perseverance, and nothing on this earth will compare to that day when we receive that Heavenly reward which will not fade because it is not of this world. It is my desire that someday I will be able to echo the words of Paul when he said in 2 Timothy 4:7, "I have fought the good fight, I have finished the race, I have kept the faith."

After the Final Buzzer with Doug Jarvis

"Each of the NHL players you've read about in this book has told his own story of perseverance, in his hockey career, as well as in his faith. The game of hockey, as well as life, is full of uncertainty. As we've seen in these stories, injuries, trades, being "called up," being "sent down," and struggles of all sorts are a regular part of the game – not to mention the pressures of fame, fortune, extreme highs when everything's going well, and devastating lows when they aren't. It's easy to see the importance of a solid foundation and a strong support system that encourages these players throughout the challenges of a professional hockey career.

"But the fact is that everyone experiences ups and downs, trials and challenges, successes and failures. Those things are not specific to a professional athlete's story. They're a part of everyone's story...mine, and yours. You may be experiencing some of the uncertainties of life right now, and if you aren't, I don't mean to be discouraging, but you will. Who will you turn to in those times? Where will you draw encouragement and find answers, not just temporary strength to get through some circumstance, but a lasting knowledge that no matter what comes your way, you will be able to persevere and to grow as a result?

"**All of the players in this book found that reassurance through a personal faith in Jesus Christ**. And, as you've seen, that faith has made them strong and courageous. They are not immune to life's difficulties, but confident and hopeful through them. That kind of faith is possible for you too.

DOUG JARVIS

On behalf of David Booth, Mike Fisher, Mike Rupp, Michael Sauer, Shane Doan, Dan Hamhuis, and B.J. Crombeen, and my colleagues at Hockey Ministries International, we thank you for taking the time to read this book, and trust that you have been inspired to persevere in the game and in life. If you want to find out more about developing a closer relationship with God through Christ, I encourage you to read the following section, Joining the Team.

Doug Jarvis

Here are some of my favorite scriptures and a few questions that might help you in thinking about how you can apply God's Word in your daily life.

Proverbs 3:5-6: *"Trust in the Lord with all your heart and lean not on your own understanding; in all your ways acknowledge him, and he will make your paths straight."*

Isaiah 40:30-31: *"Even youths grow tired and weary, and young men stumble and fall; but those who hope in the Lord will renew their strength. They will soar on wings like eagles; they will run and not grow weary, they will walk and not be faint."*

What obstacles have threatened to get in the way in your journey toward achieving your goals? What has your response been to these obstacles? What encouragement can you draw from these scriptures when you face challenging times?

What lessons have you learned throughout your life that keep you going in the face of opposition?

What are the highest priorities in your life, and how do you keep these in balance with other demands?

What does "perseverance" mean to you? How have you exhibited perseverance in your journey? From where do you draw strength to persevere?

Have you considered how keeping your focus on Jesus Christ can help you overcome obstacles and challenges and stay the course in your journey? Who encourages you in your spiritual journey?

What do you feel you need to do to build the solid foundation and strong support system that can encourage you throughout your journey toward your goal?

References

[1] "Bulletin: Senators trade Mike Fisher to Nashville for first- (2011) and third- (2012) round draft picks." Retrieved from: http://senators.nhl.com/club/news.htm?id=552268, October 2, 2011/12:43 PM/News, Ottawa Senators. (09.29.2011)

[2] "NHL Entry Draft Profile – Dan Hamhuis." Retrieved from: www.sportsnetwork.com/merge/tsnform.aspx?c=sportsnetwork&page=nhl/misc/draft-hamhuis.htm. (10.19.2011)

[3] "2002-03 Round 4/Game 7: Mike Rupp Goal – YouTube." Retrieved from: www.youtube.com/watch?v=giaCEVg3Lrg, uploaded by McKay4429061, November 5, 2008. (09.30.2011)

Joining the Team

There are thousands of hockey players, their families and fans who are struggling to find meaning in life. Maybe you are one of them. Possibly you are really caught up in the game. Hockey is our passion and livelihood, but it is not the answer to eternal hope, peace and fulfillment. It's important to think about where you place your trust and the truths upon which you are building your life. Regardless of your current relationship with Him, Jesus' love for you has no boundaries; He is there for you to guide you through your challenges on and off the ice. We encourage you to read through this special Hockey Player's New Testament. Also please take time to consider the following paragraphs which provide a brief outline on how to discover true purpose in life through a personal relationship with God.

1. God Has a Goal for each One of Our Lives

God has a goal for each of us. He wants us to live full and meaningful lives by loving and serving Him.

The Apostle Paul explained it this way:

"God has made us what we are, and in union with Christ Jesus he has created us for a life of good deeds, which he has already prepared for us to do." (Ephesians 2:10)

2. We Have All Broken God's Rules

Just like there are rules when you step onto the ice to play, there are rules to the game of life. It's God's game, it's his rink and we play by his rules... or at least we're supposed to! But we all take shortcuts with the playbook. Sometimes we want to get ahead and sometimes we just think we know better than the coach. God calls our breaking the rules by a word we don't use much anymore.

"...everyone has sinned and is far away from God's presence." *(Romans 3:23)*

3. We All Deserve God's Penalty

When you break the rules on the ice... there's a penalty. When you break God's rules for life, there's also a penalty but the consequences are much more serious. Sin pulls us away from God's perfect presence... far away and separated from God forever. The Bible sometimes calls this death.

"For sin pays it wages - death; but God's free gift is eternal life in union with Christ Jesus our Lord." *(Romans 6:23)*

Hey, that sounded like good news at the end of that verse. What's that about a free gift?

4. Our penalty has been served by a "Teammate"..

You probably already know that when a goalie breaks the rules, one of his teammates serves his time in the penalty box. Jesus, your Teammate, has served your penalty.

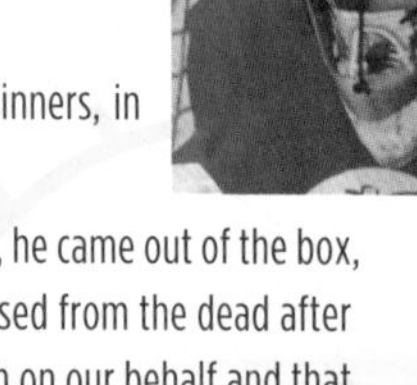

When the officials looked at Christ's on-ice performance it turns out he had never broken the rules, not a single time! Because he didn't have to serve a penalty for himself, he served yours. That's exactly what happened when Jesus died on the Cross 2000 years ago. He took your place in the penalty box.

"But God has shown us how much he loves us – it was while we were still sinners that Christ died for us!" *(Romans 5:8)*

"For Christ died for sins once and for all, a good man on behalf of sinners, in order to lead you to God." *(1 Peter 3:18)*

The added piece of good news is that after Jesus served your penalty, he came out of the box, just to prove that the penalty was paid in full. Because Jesus was raised from the dead after paying the penalty for our sins, we know that God accepted His death on our behalf and that Jesus is alive forever to skate beside us in the game of life.

5. We Have to Accept the Offer

As you consider joining God's team please understand that it does not involve a fierce struggle or competition with other players in an effort to earn a position on the team.

"For it is by grace you have been saved, through faith – and this not from yourselves, it is the gift of god – not by works, so that no one can boast." *(Ephesians 2:8,9)*

God is offering forgiveness and eternal life as a gift. You can become a part of His team by accepting His gift of forgiveness and salvation.

It's really no more complicated than telling God that you know you need Him because you can't pull this off on your own. If you have never spoken to God in prayer before, you might not quite know how to go about it. But it's really rather simple. Some people approach it like this:

> *Heavenly Father,*
> ***I know you sent Your Son, Jesus Christ into the world to be my substitute. I know I need to be forgiven. I believe that Jesus died for my sins, paid my penalty in full and rose again from the dead. I accept Him as my personal Savior and invite him to be Lord of my life. Help me turn away from wrong and learn to surrender my life to you and to live in a way that pleases you, as the Bible teaches.***

Playing on the Team

If you've decided to join the team, we'd love to hear about it. Please contact the person who gave you this New Testament or our staff at Hockey Ministries International. We would be pleased to send a copy of the booklet, The Bible and the Game of Life.

Here are some ideas as you develop in your relationship with Jesus Christ:

Find Teammates

You will struggle if you try to grow in your faith on your own. We all need friends to encourage and spur us on. Seek out a Christian church in your community that teaches the truths of the Bible. Establish friendships with like-minded believers and get involved in Bible studies and fellowship groups. *(See Hebrews 10:24)*

Talk to the Coach

Christians need to communicate with the "Head Coach" (God) through prayer. This is an essential part of the Christian life. The New Testament reminds us to always keep on praying. We can pray anywhere, anytime about anything. *(See Philippians 4:6-7)*

Trust the Coach

Just like players have to learn to trust the coach and his game plan so we have to trust the Lord and His plan for our lives. *(See Ephesians 2:10)*

Know the Playbook

God has given us His playbook (the Bible) to guide us through life. He wants us to read and study it each day and to apply its truths to our lives. It is the best way to get to know God and find peace. *(See 2 Timothy 2:15)*

Draw Strength from the Holy Spirit

When a person accepts Jesus, the Holy Spirit comes to live within him. He will strengthen and enable you to live a strong Christian life. Learn to be sensitive to His presence within you and to walk in step with His leading. *(See Galatians 5:16)*

Tell Others

Take every opportunity to tell others, especially family members, teammates and friends about your personal faith in Jesus Christ. *(See 2 Corinthians 5:18-20)*

Getting a Grip on the Bible

The Bible is our playbook for life. Benefitting from it requires planning and discipline writes Ryan Walter: "During my 15 years in the NHL I had to continuously practice my skills to stay sharp. The same is true in our spiritual lives. We have to plan and be disciplined about setting time aside daily to study God's Word."

Here are some skills that will help you to gain strength for life:

LEARN... AS YOU STUDY THE BIBLE

In Acts 17:11 and 2 Timothy 2:15 we are taught to study, making sure we understand what the Bible says. It helps to ask: "who wrote the passage?"; "to whom was it written and what is the lesson or theme?." Taking notes and memorizing important verses anchors our understanding.

LISTEN... AS GOD SPEAKS THROUGH THE BIBLE

We can improve our spiritual ears by setting aside time daily to read in a quiet location as Jesus did in Mark 1:35; developing a thirst for righteousness *(Matt. 5:6)*; desiring spiritual truth *(1 Peter 2:1,2)*; putting God first in our lives *(Matt. 6:33)*.

LIVE... AS YOU PRACTICE WHAT YOU LEARN

Jesus said: "...everyone who hears these words of mine and puts them into practice is like a wise man who built his house upon the rock."

By putting what we learn into action, we build a solid foundation for the trials of life.

LEAN... AS YOU TRUST GOD'S PROMISES

The Lord wants us to trust His promises and lean on Him through life's challenges. Jesus promises to give us rest as we come to Him *(Matt. 11:28)*.

LEAD... AS YOU SHARE BIBLE TRUTHS WITH OTHERS

Paul urged his young friend Timothy to tell others about the important truths he was learning. *(2 Timothy 2:2)*.

Where eternity meets the ice

"Today church is not restricted to a dwelling or a building; it's much more fluid than that. At Hockey Ministries International ("HMI"), church is sometimes a rink, a locker room, a hotel lobby or a personal encounter on the ice."
– Glen "Chico" Resch, Color Analyst for the New Jersey Devils; former All-Star NHL Goaltender and Stanley Cup champion.

Rooted in their Christian faith and their love for the game of hockey, HMI is an active hockey family working year-round to conduct camps, chapels and special events, and to produce publications and other media communicating the message of Hope found in Jesus Christ.

From Humble Beginnings

Forty years ago, working his way through the ranks of junior and then professional hockey, one young player felt quite alone in his Christian faith. Keenly aware of the demands the game imposes on players and their families, he recognized a glaring void in players' lives left by the absence of any meaningful moral or spiritual support systems.

He felt the need for a dimension of hope and faith among his teammates and opponents, their families, friends and fans. But hockey's demanding schedules – practices, games and travel – make it almost impossible for players to attend a familiar community church on a regular basis. And many fans sought fulfillment at the rink rather than at church. What could be done? How could this hockey culture benefit from the answers found in the Christian faith? How could the Hope that he knew be brought to the rink?

Where eternity meets the ice

In 1977, the first seeds were sown in the form of a Christian hockey camp for youth in Montreal. That first year Christian NHL and CFL players provided instruction on ice and in dry land sports. They also explained how their faith helped them in their careers and personal lives; and how a spiritual support system can help prepare you for life's challenges. Campers learned that being a Christian gives you guidance for issues that arise each day and hope for your future. It's about courage, perseverance, teamwork and trophies that last forever.

HMI's first camp was a small one, but big enough to form the foundation of everything that HMI is today. Since the 1970's a Christian movement has been growing throughout hockey communities in North America and in other countries around the world as players and fans have taken up the cause together.

The Spirit of HMI . . .

Perhaps our core programs, camps and chapels, best exemplify the spirit of HMI. Every summer HMI hosts 30 week-long Christian Hockey Camps in 6 different countries, Canada, USA, Sweden, Switzerland, Slovakia and the Czech Republic. Over 600 volunteers, including NHL players and coaches, give their time each summer to make these camps happen. Training programs blend physical, mental and spiritual conditioning, preparing players for challenges on and off the ice. Morning and evening chapels feature youth-oriented music programs, inspirational testimony and opportunities to talk with the pros. Humour, practical jokes and fun are an important part of the mix. Professional players, coaches and counsellors provide positive role models that remain with the young players long after camp ends. David Booth, Left Wing for the Florida Panthers has this to say: "Every year I coach at 1 or 2 camps. God has given me a gift to play this game and to give the glory back to Him through the game. I know I have a great opportunity to share my faith because when I was little, I looked up to everyone who played in the NHL. I am certain the kids at camp feel the same way. You see kid's lives change at every camp – that's why we are here. Matthew 28:19 says 'Therefore go and make disciples of all nations'. I've been to camps in Canada, Czech Republic, Slovakia, Switzerland and now Florida. Everywhere, HMI is doing it for the glory of God."

An American Hockey League referee talks about the impact of a week at camp:

"My earliest memories of HMI are as a camper in the early 1990s in Saskatchewan. Under pros like Roger Neilson and Bob Bassen we learned about hockey, teamwork, and what it means to be a Christian athlete. Now that hockey has become my life and career, I cherish the valuable lessons I learned as an HMI camper and use them everyday both at and away from the rink.
– Zac Wiebe, AHL Referee

HMI's chapel programs are another way of bringing our message of Hope to the arena. Active in 30 different North American and European hockey leagues at the college, junior and professional levels, HMI's chapels engage 230 chaplains who meet with players and coaches on a regular basis to help them develop their own support network and to facilitate a consistent worship time. Meetings include a brief message and a prayer time, and provide an opportunity for players to talk about what is going on in their own lives, things that matter to them, things they struggle with and how to take hold of Biblical principles that can point their lives and careers in the right direction. As NHL Veteran and HMI Missionary Leader Laurie Boschman puts it, "a player who exercises his spiritual muscles first can benefit both himself and his teammates." Here is one coach's perspective on chapels:

"Every team I have coached has been fortunate enough to be involved with HMI. During the course of the season, there are many obstacles that we, as players and coaches, must deal with. I have found that the players I have coached and enjoyed the ability to talk to someone outside the organization. I believe that HMI provides hope and guidance."

– Ray Edwards, Head Coach of the AHL San Antonio Rampage

. . . and more . . .

> Each year HMI hosts a Breakfast during the NHL All-Star weekend, and increasingly at other major hockey events and tournaments. Fans hear players share heart-felt stories about their ups and downs, dreams and hopes, and their personal relationship with Jesus Christ, who they trust to help shepherd their future.

> HMI also organizes special Conferences, Hockey and Golf Tournaments for players and Faith Nights for fans at professional and junior games.

> In association with other Christian organizations HMI produces Videos and Literature of faith stories of hockey players.

> HMI works with the NHL Players' Association "Goals and Dreams" program to provide hockey equipment for young hockey players in places like the Czech Republic, Slovakia and Kazakhstan.

How You Can Be Involved

Since the 1970's HMI has been a growing community dedicated to supporting thousands of players, their families, friends and fans. Further expansion hinges on the passion of interested people who recognize the far-reaching impact of Christian faith, hope and unity on those who live in the demanding world of hockey. For forty years, as a result of their involvement in the HMI family, thousands of hockey players have found fulfillment and rewards beyond their wildest dreams.

Please see HMI's web site at www.hockeyministries.org for opportunities or for more details on our ministry programs.

And if you are going to be at the rink anyways, why not consider meeting someone from Hockey Ministries International.

NOUVEAU TESTAMENT du

JOUEUR DE HOCKEY

s le but

HOCKEY PLAYER'S

NEW TESTAMENT

Toward the goal

CHCI co
more th
combin

Dedicated Camp Cou

Our volunteer counselors are ca
Christian Hockey Camps Interna
parents seriously. We want to e
experience for each participant

Dry-Land Training

All Campers receive a "Pre-ca
prior to camp. Developing pov
are the highlights of our progr
demonstrated so that they ca
helps the players maximize th
highly effective on the ice. Ou
to continue growing as hocke
their departure from camp.

Cross training is critical for t
Campers will enjoy other ca
basketball, and floor hockey

APPLICATION FORM

Online registration available at: www.hockeyministries.org

FREE MEN'S SIZE Jersey for all campers: S M L XL XXL (circle size)
For goalies with oversized equipment: 2XL

1st Choice Location ______ Dates ______
2nd Choice Location ______ Dates ______
Name (Please Print) ______
Address ______
City ______ Prov/State ______ Code ______
Camper e-mail ______

Age at camp ______
ale
where possible) ______
t ______
Forward **Goalie**
Level played ______
ing Camper
etes **Epilepsy** **Allergies**

spaper Ad **Internet**

Dad **Guardian**

order for the balance dated a

to the camper fee.
erCard
piration Date ______
Amount ______

CHRISTIAN HOCKEY CAMPS
INTERNATIONAL

2012
OUR 36TH YEAR!

INTERNATIONAL HOCKEY PROGRAM AND TRAINING IN CHRISTIAN LIVING

LIVE-IN & DAY CAMPS FOR AGES 9-17

www.hockeyministries.org camps@hockeyministries.org